The Universal Antidote

It is the Cure to all problems

My presence is the solution to all problems, and my absence is the cause.

What am I?

Also By

E.K. Bempoh

Perception

Is it not wise?

Riddle, Riddle

Indication to Eternal Destination

The Universal Antidote

E.K. Bempoh

References

This section titled "References" will allow for the location of each antidote and immunity to each problem written in this book. To find the antidotes to a problem, simply look on the left side of this section. The Antidotes to each problem listed on the left side of this page (References) will begin with the problem, followed by the letter "A" for "Antidote", and if there are more than one antidotes, that number will be listed after A, after the antidote, you will see a dash like so "-" and you will see the letter "P" for "Page" followed by the page number. So, for example, if you wanted to look up the first antidote for sickness, you would look for "Sickness A1- P3" on the left side of the "References" section which is what you're reading at the moment. You will follow the same procedure for "Immunities" but you will see "I" for immunities instead of "A" and immunities will be located on the right side.

Antidotes:	Immunities:
Sickness A1: p50	Sickness I1: p40
Fear A1: 63	Sickness I1: p44
Fear A2: p65	Fear I1 & I2: p71
Unforgiveness A1: p76	Unforgiveness I1: p80
Unforgiveness A2: p78	Unforgiveness I2: p81
Sin(General) A1:p100	Premature Death I1: p88
Sin(General) A2:p103	Premature Death I2: p91
Sin(General) A3:p106	Premature Death I3: p92
	Premature Death I4: p93

The Cure

Pre-knowledge

———

The relevance of evil is a major prerogative in the defense of many atheistic arguments. Many who argue against the existence of God rarely fail to introduce the intrusion of evil in the world, and further tend to question why God would allow it, if he truly exists. It tends to defy the logic of many why a God deemed good, righteous, and just, would allow evil to possess the world. It is always easier to blame another rather than ourselves as a result of our sinful and fleshly nature as people who have had the privilege of wearing a body. As time continues to deliver the order of our choices, we may come to the understanding that the world operates by principle and is governed by the law of Justification. Those who are given the gift of life on earth express their will within the boundaries of the world due to the temporarily permanent habitation. The world expresses its nature within the boundaries of certain laws placed by God during creation in order for all hosts to operate without failure. All things created were created to exist for a particular reason, and therefore will only express that innate nature untampered. Birds fly, Dogs bark, Fish swim. These are all innate expressions of the nature of living creations. God created the earth to follow the principle of exchange. Everything that was created has

———

exchanged, is exchanging, and will continue to exchange. This is one of the Governing principles of life. In order for a manifestation to proceed, there must be an exchange somewhere because things don't just happen without causing other things to happen. Anything done may have been done at the expense of another and that is the foundation of the birth of choice. The problem many face is when given the choice to choose, we may fail to recognize or perceive right, therefore choosing to do without certainty of accuracy, which often may result in unwanted outcomes we call problems. Luckily in life, there is a cure to all problems, a cure to consequence, it is the universal antidote.

Problems

A problem could be described as failure to operate as expected or simply an obstacle that prevents the achievement of a desired outcome. All plans are subject to failure because of the unpredictable nature of indefinite events that occur. Most if not all problems are derived from one source; Ignorance. If we were all perfect in knowledge, we would incur little to no problems. Now here's how problems are birthed in many cases. There is a goal that is to be achieved, and in order to achieve this goal you need information. Assuming you've gathered the necessary information you need to achieve your desired outcome, all you need to do is implement it. Now there are several stages of subsequent possibilities that may cause a problem to immerge. If after implementation of the necessary knowledge, you achieve your goal, then your knowledge base must have been pretty accurate. But if you encounter a problem along your implementation process, the root cause of your problem is most certainly the lack of certain knowledge. Now it doesn't matter how much we think we know, there is always more knowledge to be acquired. Problems are inevitable in the context of both the lack of knowledge and failure to have access to the source of all knowledge. If ever failure is encountered, it is because there is certain information you may be lacking, so the wisest option to avoid failure is seek as much information and knowledge as you can about your specific goal before you begin to achieve it. Now, sometimes failure is good. In fact, many success stories derived from the failure. You see, if you've ever failed at something, and later on succeeded to achieve that goal, it is because you most definitely learned something. So sometimes failure was designed to create an opportunity to attain certain information you may not have been likely to easily attain, and therefore allowing you to acquire exactly what you need to succeed. So, don't be afraid of failure, it is only there to show us we lack knowledge, and to help us gain the knowledge we lack.

Solutions

——

For every representation of good, there is a counterpart represented as evil. This is due to the existence of a law called the law of opposites. The law of opposites simply states all things in specified context that express a certain function are likely to have a counterpart that expresses the same function in opposite context. In simplest terms, this law announces the existence of an opposite to all things. You could consider the possibility that anything bad is simply a corrupt good, and therefore all good things have the potential to be bad and all bad things could be traced back to good. A more common analogy is simply to consider the fact that all counterfeit money would be of no account if there was no original. The power of anything fake is only able to be effectual because there is an original. So, the goal of the original is to have something to tell it apart from the fake. So, for everything bad, there is a good and for everything good, the only way to make it bad is to corrupt it. Corruption is simply failure to operate as intended, or something that is no longer suitable for use. Anything that does not operate as it was created to, may be described as corrupt. This is why it is common to say, "the food has gone bad", simply because it is no longer suitable for use, it is no longer eligible to be eaten. So as per the law of opposites, if there is a problem, there is a solution. You see, this law exists to maintain what we call a balance. In life, there must be balance, and if there's ever a time there is a missing space not filled,

——

the Law of balance would cause conflict to be the placeholder until whatever is missing is filled by its rightful owner, only then will conflict leave. You see, we must come to understand that conflict is only present in the absence of balance. You see, there's a law called the law of balance, and this law is backed by the subsequent law of exchange. Everything we do in life is an exchange, and whenever we give, we aren't just giving, but we're also involved in the art of receiving. At this moment, you're giving your time and attention, and you're receiving informational knowledge. Now the law of balance is responsible for several things including the existence of light and darkness, of good and bad, of right and wrong, of sin and righteousness and more. Remember, the devil did not cause sin, he did not invent sin, he was only one of the first few creations to have been a victim of it. The possibility of sin exists because of the governing law of balance. So, when someone receives something, and does not give back the measure of which was received, it causes an imbalance, and because there is a law that exists responsible for keeping balance in motion, conflict is sent to fill in the spot of whatever was missing, until that spot is filled its rightful owner. In other words, peace is the result of balance, but whenever you spot conflict, someone has not received whatever they should have received. So, if there is conflict in a marriage, it is simply suggesting the reality that someone in that marriage is not giving something that they should be giving. There is one major law called the law of vacancy. This law simply states, no space can be truly empty. All space must have a host. And so, God created the heavens and the earth, and assigned hosts to each as per the law of vacancy. We were created to fulfill this law by living here, and the angelic amongst other creations fulfil this law by living in the heavens. This law is the reason nothing can be truly empty. So, whenever you see a cup that has nothing in it, and you label it empty, it simply shows the limited capacity of our eyes to see air. Is it not a wonder that exactly what we need to live is exactly what we fail to see? Now, the moment we poor water into an empty cup, air leaves immediately. So, on this planet, anything we call empty is actually full of air, and until that space is filled or replaced with another content, the air will remain. So whenever something leaves, something else must fill that space in order to keep balance going, and if nothing feels that space it would cause an imbalance, and so conflict must come to fill that space not only to maintain balance, but as a sign that there is something missing that should be present, as a sign that there is a space that needs to be filled. So, problems are a sign of conflict, which means there is a space of knowledge that must be filled, and therefore as per the law of opposites, must have a solution.

The Cure

Knowledge

——

My presence is the solution to all problems, and my absence is the cause. What am I? The answer is knowledge. The cure and antidote to any problem non-contingent is certain knowledge. Now, in the realms of knowledge, there is much to be known. Everything is a form of knowledge. You were created by knowledge, and everything around you is a product of knowledge. Existence itself is the reality of the collection of knowledge. It is responsible for the all-inclusive expression of diverse knowledge into reality. In the realm of time of which inhabits the earth, there is a certain limit of knowledge we are enabled to attain. You see, when God created man, just as he set a limit on how far and low the clouds are allowed to go (Job 38, 9-10), he set a limit on the level of knowledge man is able to attain access (2 Corinthians 12:4). Our natural capacity for knowledge is limited, and there are certain things we are not allowed to know. This is simply why we call certain things impossible, yet to God, they are very easily possible. You see, if we had access to certain knowledge of which we have no legal permission to access, we would be able to do all the things we see as impossible now. That's what Faith in God is. Faith in God is simply acknowledging yourself as a creation, therefore putting into effect the realization that God is perfect in knowledge while accepting we are not, and allowing the restriction of his righteous nature to make you at peace with leaving all things in his hands, and blindly believing he will do it.

——

Faith is letting go of what we think we know and trusting in God with perfect knowledge to do what we can't do with limited knowledge. So, every habitation of creation has a restriction of knowledge they are allowed to deliver to those who reside in them. The earth has a specified capacity of knowledge it is allowed to entertain. Given the context of those who have received salvation from Jesus Christ, we are given access into new knowledge. There are dimensions and levels of knowledge that open up new possibilities the moment you gain access. So, you may have come to operate in the gift of the spirit because you attained certain knowledge, or you can drive because you attained certain knowledge. You may be able to cook because you attained certain knowledge, and you may be able to start, head, and sustain a successful business because you attained certain knowledge. Nevertheless, it doesn't matter how much knowledge a creation has been able to attain, there is a limit, and limit is one of the major differences between God and Man. It was the tree of knowledge of good and evil that Adam was commanded not to eat. You see, knowledge is so powerful that when we receive unauthorized access to it, it may cause corruption and more problems than good. This is what was seen with Adam and Eve pertaining to the tree of the knowledge of good and evil. So, sometimes it is wise to take the immunity of obedience in order to escape the consequence of ignorance. If Adam had refrained from certain knowledge, things would have been much different for us today. It is wise to heed to the counsel that expresses the importance of acknowledging the reality that access to certain knowledge may cause more problems. Sometimes ignorance is only allowed in Obedience. If God commanded his human creation not to steal, we may not always need to know why, we just need to obey. So, obedience is the antidote to the consequence of ignorance. We must come to the acknowledgment of God's description of perfection in the similitude of what exists to be knowledge. Doing so will allow us to have greater access to God dimension- Knowledge. You see there is a spirit called the spirit of knowledge. The spirit of knowledge is responsible for displaying the nature of God's knowledge at a dimension to the host. If you wish to attain the benefit of this spirit of knowledge in greater dimensions than others, you must begin by acknowledging that despite the amount of knowledge you may have acquired, there is still far more than that which exists in the realm of asking or thinking, and the legal way to get it, is from God. You may soon come to realize that money follows after one thing; It follows packaged knowledge. Everything your money will ever buy (contingent) is packaged knowledge. So, when you buy a new car it is simply someone's knowledge of transportation you purchased. When you buy a cell phone, it is someone's knowledge of communication you've purchased. It is very important to understand the value of knowledge and how it relates to our lives, it is then that we will see a high and consistent level of success in our lives.

The Cure

Note: The following quantifications are the generalization of indefinite validations in the realm of current knowledge eligible for access at the time of this writing, and therefore may be subject to addition in certain inferences per knowledge growth. All text, ideas, and theories in this book (excluding bible references) are the original work of the author, All Rights Reserved.

Quantifications

<u>3 Classifications of all Problems</u>:

All problems may be quantified into three classifications. The Problems of the Spirit, Soul, and Body. We are all made up of trinomial components that work together to form one singularity known as the creation of Man. Genesis 2:7 reveals the formation of Man and the ingredient that brought the formed dust to life; The spirit. You see, the body was formed on the earth by the ingredients of the earth, and the spirit is the breath of God, meaning it is a substance of God, a piece of an essence of God that is eternal, and the combination of spiritual substance(spirit), and physical substance(body) is what caused us to have living souls. The Living soul of man was the result of combining eternity with time. It is responsible for relaying and transmitting information from one realm to the other. It is the bridge of reception and transmission from the spirit to body for execution in the physical realm. So, we are not specifically and only a body, we only have a body to operate the executions of God on earth. The soul may commonly be known by many to host our mind, emotions and will. So, any problem we incur will either be a problem of the spirit, a problem of the soul, and a problem of the body because those are the expressions of ourselves that interact with the realms made known to us; The spiritual and the physical, or the seen and unseen realms. The problems of the body may often directly affect the body such as physical sickness. The problems of the soul may often directly affect the soul such as fear. And the problems of the spirit may often directly affect the spirit, such as the lack of discernment, prayerlessness, demonic oppression, etc... So, we must be able to recognize what aspect of our being is being affected by any problem we encounter, this will help us cure the problem effectively.

2 types of all problems

Now, we've come to discover that all problems have 3 recipients, meaning all problems we will have can either affect the spirit, soul, and/or body. Now, to go even further, there are 2 types of problems; Universal problems, and Contingent Problems. Universal problems are problems that can affect all three entities of our being; the spirit, soul, and body such as hunger. Now hunger itself is not a problem under the condition that it is a righteous hunger. But hunger can bring problems if it is not satisfied. Hunger was designed to be a sign of health, as well as a sign that there is space for an addition, and so hunger will always need to be satisfied, and in the case where it isn't, that is where it becomes a problem. There is a principle called the principle of likeness. This principle simply states that if one element of a like substance to another expresses a particular function, then the other element of similar substance is likely to have certain trait in similitude to the other. For example, the mango fruit grows from a tree, and therefore if an apple is found to be a fruit like the mango, then it is likely to have developed in a similar way as the mango, in which case both the apple and the mango grow from trees. Though they are different in expression, they are both in the fruit category, and because of that, they both grow from trees. So, though the spirit, soul, and body maybe different entities and may express themselves differently, they all have similar traits, and therefore are subject to the principle of likeness. So, with this principle in motion, if the body is able to get hungry, then it is likely that the soul and spirit could also experience hunger as well, usually in a metaphorical sense. You see, the spirit came from God, and that is why the bible declares us to worship God in spirit and truth, because God himself is spirit. Now, the body was designed to eat physical food, the soul was designed to eat information, and engaging in things like prayer, worship, reading the word are things that feed the spirit. So, all three of our trinomial makeup are subject to hunger, and the consequences of the hunger of the body are known to some. But do we know what the consequences of the hunger of the soul? Ignorance is one of the greatest consequences and reactions of starving our soul. A consequence of starving our spirit is simply the reduction of awareness to the spiritual realm. God communicates to us through our spirit, so it is crucial that we feed our spirits. Contingent problems are problems that are contingent on a particular entity of our being. These problems could only affect either the soul, body, or spirit, but not all 3.

2 Originations of all Problems:

Now the problem many times tend to lie in the fact that we often encounter a problem of the body for example, and automatically by the influence of ignorance think the problem originated from the realm of the physical, while in fact sometimes problems that directly affect the body may have originated from the Spirit realm. So, we should not only consider what the problem directly affects, but also what realm the problem may have originated from. There are two realms of which all problems we may encounter on earth originate from; The spiritual realm, and the physical realm. What we must come to know is that the physical realm is the product of the spiritual realm. God created first the spiritual realm, then gave birth to the physical realm (Genesis 1:1). To influence the physical, it is only wise to make a change in the spiritual realm first, then time will deliver that manifestation in the physical. This is because the spiritual realm is greater than the physical realm. It is not only the first realm God created, but it is an eternal realm. All things pertaining to the spirit are eternal because God is spirit, and he is eternal, therefore because he is the father of spirits, all spirits are eternal as well. Now here's the key point. It doesn't necessarily matter where the problem originates, it can always be cured by the laws of the spirit realm. So, whether you encounter a physical problem or a spiritual problem, it can be cured by the laws of the spirit. Both the physical realm and the spiritual realm are governed by laws and principles of which they operate from. This is how Jesus was able to walk on water. There is a physical law of gravity that suggests the reality that portrays the effect of sinking if anyone should step into deep water, but a higher law of the spiritual realm overruled the lesser law of the physical realm, allowing Jesus to succeed in walking on water. The physical laws can only cure physical problems, but spiritual laws can cure both physical and spiritual problems. So, we must be able to recognize the realm of which our problems originate, that will help us find an effectual cure and show us where to look for a solution. Lastly, just as we have two parents responsible for our birth; A mother and a father, all humans can be traced back to a woman. Just as we have the spiritual realm and the physical realm, all problems may be traced back the spiritual realm.

4 Categories of all problems:

Now, before we begin, it Is very important for you to know that all problems are the exact and direct result of the lack of fulfilling a need. I have come to the conclusion that there are 4 needs we must meet and failing to do so is what causes the problems we may encounter. So, my conclusion simply expresses the point that all problems fall under 4 categories, and these 4 categories are 4 needs we all need to meet and failing to meet one of more of these needs may create a substantial amount of problems. The 4 categories are; Place, Companionship, Operation and Satisfaction.

Place: Many people face certain problems based on the place they find themselves. An example would be racism. Racism is a problem of place. You may find that in Africa, there is little to no racism because it is a place with a majority of blacks, but in the U.S racism may find way to be expressed more easily simply because the country of America hosts a majority of white Americans. So, certain issues may arise because of the place an individual may be. Be sure to note that place can also be metaphoric in certain scenarios, but this inference refers to a more literal sense. You may notice that the first thing God did after creating Adam was to plant a garden in Eden, and place Adam there (Genesis 2:8). For every season and chapter in your life, there is a place you should be, and sometimes being in the wrong place regardless of time both right and wrong may be the cause of certain problems. Any problem that could be avoided by a change of place or environment would fall under this category.

Operation: All creations were created to express a particular function, and failure to do so as well as anything that may be an obstacle in fulfilling that operation is what we may call a problem. A fish was made to swim, and failure to operate in that function relays the message of a problem. There are many examples of problems that fit into this category, but a major one is sickness. Your heart was designed to pump blood around your body, the eyes were designed to provide sight, the ears were designed to accommodate hearing, your entire body was designed to function a particular way, so whenever there is sickness, it prohibits your body from functioning as it should and therefore would be recognized as a problem. Joblessness also falls under this category. You may notice that God placed Adam in the garden for the purpose of taking care of it (Genesis 2:15). That was his job. That was his operation. We all have an original operation. We have an assignment to manifest on earth, and failure to do just that may be the cause of many problems. Any area of your life that seems to be out of original and intended function would be in this category.

Companionship: After God settled Adam in the garden with his purpose and comfort in actualization, he made a profound statement. God made mention that it is not good for the man to be alone (Genesis 2:18). For God to make such a statement as the one mentioned here; "not good", it means God has foreseen a set of problems Adam may encounter by remaining alone, and by wisdom, he made a companion for him. He actually brought her out of him for the purposes of which he made known. God created both (male and female) to be represented as (man) to portray his image and likeness (Genesis 1:27). Now, please note that the bible used the word "alone" not "lonely". There is a difference here. Adam was not lonely, he was alone, and therefore he was in need of a physical companion. So, God put him to sleep, and took out of him his rib(or some part of him) and formed the woman (Genesis 2:21-22). So, the word declares "She shall be called woman, because she was taken out of man" (Genesis 2:23). You may notice in Genesis, when Adam is the reference, the bible will often say "the man", but when there's reference of both man and woman represented by the singular pronoun of him, it will often say "man". So, eve was taken out of man(Him) and that created the new pronoun; Them(because Man no longer had one representation(Adam) but two (Adam and Eve)). And so, the bible declares "So God created man in his own image, in the image and likeness of God he created him; male and female he created them" (Genesis 1:27AMP). Take notice the bible uses the word "man" (the combination of both male and female) to portray his imag' reason may be because God is The Father, The Son, and the Holy Spirit, and all his dimensions still function in one office and as one God. So, though God is God and can do all things, he makes known the importance of companionship. There are many problems we face because we have no companions, we have no people to associate with, and that may lead to unwanted outcomes. Many people fail because they don't have certain people to help them succeed, while on the flip side, many people fail because there are certain people in their lives that tear down their dreams and hinder them from achieving their goals. It is very important to know and be cautions of those you allow to be companions in your life. It did not end very well for Samson because of this issue. Sometimes, how far you may go in life may be linked to the kind of people you have around your life, so let it be that you should not be alone, but have companions as Jesus did, and choose your companions carefully, as Jesus did.

Satisfaction: Failure to fulfill this need is cause of many problems, especially those of lust. Hunger creates the space for satisfaction. When we get physically hungry, we often seek satisfaction. It's a principle, hunger allows space for addition or acquisition. Whenever there is hunger, it is a sign that there is space for addition. Hunger is an invitation to acquisition. So, there are many problems we encounter simply because of the lack of satisfaction. An example would be cheating or divorce. If there is cheating in a relationship, it is most likely the result of dissatisfaction. The person doing the cheating may not have been satisfied in a particular area in the relationship. Any form of cheating whether in a relationship, or during a test can be rooted to a satisfaction problem and will fall under this category. A problem such as disobedience would fall under this category. Anytime someone commits disobedience, it simply means they are not satisfied with the conditions of obedience. So many problems, including those of insufficiencies may be the result of dissatisfaction, and may fall under this category. This was the cause of sin. After God Placed Adam In the garden, and gave him the operation of keeping his garden, he then gave him a companion (Eve). Likewise, Eve was given a place (The garden), an operation (to help Adam), and a companion (Adam). But after all this, what caused them to sin? What caused them to disobey God? Dissatisfaction. They weren't satisfied with what they had. They wanted more knowledge, they wanted knowledge that would make them "wise like God". It was the lack of Satisfaction that caused sin to invade, and therefore death to prevail, but thanks to our Lord Jesus Christ, we are no longer slaves to such a law.

2 Resolutions of all problems:

Now in the realm of problems, we can classify resolutions into 2. Immunities, and cures/antidotes. Immunities are things we can do to prevent a problem from occurring. Antidotes are things we do to get rid of problems after we encounter them, just in case they were not prevented. In life you can either prevent a possibility or change it. If we can't prevent a problem, the next step is to cure it, and if we don't want to have to cure a problem, then the wisest choice is to prevent it. So, immunities were designed to prevent and isolate a person from the path of problems, while cures and antidotes were designed to remove a problem from a person's life.

The Bempoh Quantification Tree of All Problems

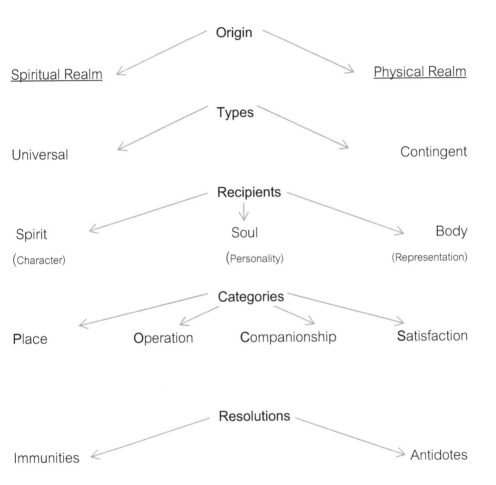

Origin

Spiritual Realm → → Physical Realm

Types

Universal ← → Contingent

Recipients

Spirit ← Soul → Body

(Character) (Personality) (Representation)

Categories

Place ← Operation ← Companionship → Satisfaction

Resolutions

Immunities ← → Antidotes

Note: Explanation of tree on back page

Summarized Explanation of quantification tree

The Hierarchical quantification tree of all problems summarizes the point that all problems originate from either the spiritual or physical realm. This is because of the law of origin which states that all things have an origin that may have been founded in a plane of habitation called a place, or an area of location, a realm that is able to host creations. The types of problems are made evident on the next step down after origin to depict the quantification of all problems into restricted and unrestricted effect. This simply shows that there are problems that affect all recipients, and are called universal problems, while there are problems that affect only one or two out of the three recipients called contingent problems. The tree moves on to depict the idea that all problems can affect either our spirit, soul, or body. This is because in order for there to be a problem, there has to be an interaction of two elements, one of the receiving end, and one on the giving end. So, a problem leaves a point of origin and meets a recipient to find expression. So, in terms of the creation of man, because we have three entities that make up our person, the problems could engage any of the three. The tree continues by categorizing all problems into four; Place, Operation, Companionship, and Satisfaction. This simply explains the idea that all problems are caused by the impact of those four functions, and all possibilities of problems one may encounter will be derived out of one of more of the four categorizations. Now, out of

34

the possibilities of problems that could occur, there are two modes of resolutions. One responsible for preventing we ourselves from crossing the path of certain problems and the other responsible for getting rid of a problem if encountered.

The Cure

Major problems

Now, there are many problems we may encounter throughout our lives, some of which we could not have had the advantage to predict, but below are some major and common problems we may encounter under each category. Please note, that some problems may also fall under one or more of these four categories. Any problem that may fall under more than one of the four categories below can be referred to as a Uni-sourced problem.

Note: Some problems may fit in one or more categories than those of which they are placed under in certain contexts, the goal here is simply to emphasize the idea of Majority. These problems are placed under the categories of which they originate from the most.

Place	Operation	Companionship	Satisfaction
Sickness.	Sickness	Loneliness	Lust
Inequality	Unemployment	Disobedience	Inequality
Unemployment	Disappointment	Fear	Disobedience
Lack	Poverty	(PD)	Unforgiveness
Fear	Lack		Ignorance
Poverty	Fear		Lying
(PD)	Homosexuality		Fear
	Premature Death(PD)		

The Cure

Antidotes & Immunities

_____

The next few pages will host the immunities and antidotes of a few major problems as it pertains to the kingdom of God. This means, all antidotes and immunities will be kingdom resolutions backed and validated by the written word of God; The bible and therefore will operate by kingdom laws and principles.

The Cure

Sickness

———

Recipients:

This represents the specific entity of our being that may be affected by the problem of sickness.

|| Spirit - Soul - **Body**

Area of Focus:

This represents the specific entity we will focus on providing the antidote to as well as the immunity to prevent.

|| Body sickness

Category:

Place, Operation

Immunity:

Now, this is quite a popular and highly common problem. At some point, most if not all people without the help of supernatural power have fallen sick. In the entirety of Jesus's life, it was not heard that he fell sick, in fact he took it 2 steps further and healed the sick. So, what is this power that prevented Jesus from falling sick, and rather allowing him to not only heal the sick but

———

to take all our sickness away by his stripes (Isaiah 53:5). Did you know you could have food in front of you and still be hungry? or be completely inside water and be thirsty? Jesus came to do many things on earth, and amongst which he took our sicknesses away. The moment he took our sin, and fulfilled his destiny, he restored the order of which God made it to be in the beginning, that includes the absence of sickness. Did you know there is a power responsible for preventing sickness from touching your body? Why do many have eyes, yet see not? Or ears, yet hear not? It is the blindness and deafness of ignorance. Now, the bases of operating in the kingdom and the minimum requirement for pleasing God is faith. This means faith is one of the immunities responsible for preventing sickness. It is the bases and fuel of what will be used to as an immunity to prevent this enemy of man known to be sickness. The bible declares, faith comes by hearing and hearing by the word of God (2 Corinthians 5:17). This means ignorance is an enemy of faith in many contexts. Faith expresses itself in greater measure by knowledge and information. If the bible declares faith comes by hearing by the word of God, it means faith comes by information and knowledge. The word of God; The written word (Bible), the spoken word (All things by prophecy), and the living word (Jesus) active now through the holy spirit all bring information and knowledge to us for many reasons including the growth of faith. So, you need to have knowledge in order to have faith. Faith comes by knowledge in several contexts as has been revealed here. Now, please note, there are many ways to receive healing, and there are many immunities with God, but just a few will be listed in this book.

Immunity of Faith by the hearing of the word:

Now, to those in the category of man (both male and female humans), all have been given a measure of faith. To some was the gift of faith also given. This is not our regular measure of faith distributed by the sovereignty of he who is I am, but this is an impartation of what is commonly known as the God type of faith. Those privileged to operate in this gift of faith may be more likely to use this method as an immunity to sickness. Now, the best way to activate immunity to sickness by faith is to begin by reading scriptures about the removal of sickness from our life through Jesus Christ our Lord.

❖ Begin by first getting your faith up. Faith can increase, and in order to increase your faith, you must feed your spirit. Faith is of the spirit, and therefore it will come from the spirit. The higher your faith is, the better it will work to protect you against sickness. You can get your faith up by asking God to increase your faith in prayer or ask him to give you the gift of faith and allow it to be operational in your life in higher measure. After doing this, I recommend speaking in tongues regularly and consistently. Speaking in tongues allows you to grow in the spirit, and it exercises your spiritual senses, this can help you grow in faith. The larger your spirit, the larger your faith, the larger your flesh, the greater your doubt because doubt is of the flesh and faith is of the spirit, remember that. The bible declares faith comes by hearing and hearing by the word of God. So, praying in tongues will help you develop your hearing in the spirit in order to hear God, and what God will tell you will bring faith, because prophecy is the spoken word of God, and the bible declares faith comes by hearing. Another way to get your faith up is to read the written word of God. The combination of reading the word of God and praying in the spirit is crucial for maximum growth in faith.

Make sure to do this consistently, it is through consistency that the spirit can grow at maximum efficiency and therefore faith as well. I strongly encourage every believer to pray in tongues, but if you don't, that is fine as well. If you can pray in the spirit, I encourage you to begin to pray for just 10 minutes every day for 1 month and see the results you'll actualize. You can boost the growth of your spirit and faith by fasting. Fast your spirit, soul, and body. Take 1 day in a month to begin with, and refrain from eating for 12 hours, and in that 12 hours, pray in tongues for as long as you can (you may pray in English as well), and read the word of God as well as worship him through music as well as other things, make sure to refrain from all media that has little to nothing to do with God during this period, this will boost the growth of your spirit significantly if practiced.

❖ Use the shield of Faith. You must understand that faith is many things, one of which is a shield. Faith can be used as a shield as declared in Ephesians 6:16. You can use it to protect against sickness. To begin, simply pray a prayer of Faith by declaration. After you've grown in faith, read Mark 11:24, and make a declaration. Mark 11:24 simply states, "Therefore I tell you, whatever you ask for in prayer, believe that you have received it, and it will be yours". So, all you have to do is exchange your faith for God's power of immunity from sickness. It's quite simple. Go to God, and ask him to keep sickness from you, and believe he has done it! This is where you'll know how great your faith is. If you have doubt, you need to quench it and exercise your faith even more by the things I listed above and pray again. After you pray God should keep sickness from you, and that any sickness that touches your body must die instantly, declare this, "I declare, no sickness shall touch my body in Jesus Name". Declare it or any declaration of faith concerning your immunity to sickness, and believe what you have prayed and declared, and it shall be done In Jesus Name.

❖ Personal Testimony: Freshman year of college the season brought winter and I lived in a 4-member suite. My roommate and I on one side, and 2 suite mates on the other, and we had a bathroom connecting us, so all four of shared the same bathroom. During this winter, I happened to be quite active in prayer and It came to my notice my faith had grown since before I became consistent in prayer and reading his word. So, during this winter my roommate had caught a cold, and so did my suite mates. I on the other hand noticed how the cold was spreading not just in my dorm room but throughout the university, so I decided to use mark 11:24 to pray and make a declaration. I prayed that no sickness will touch my body, and I declared, then I followed that prayer and declaration with a few minutes of prayer in tongues, and that was done. I believed everything I prayed and declared, and I believed if a sickness touched my skin, it would die. My faith was so strong that as my roommate coughed and sneezed it did not move me; I had no fear at all. It became such a big deal that my roommate wondered why I wasn't sick. I used the same bathroom, same sink, same room, we both go out to the same cold, many people were sick, all the suite mates were sick, and yet I remained untouched, and I wasn't doing anything special, I wasn't protecting myself, I had such faith, I would touch him and his things, I would sometimes go out without heavy protection and still nothing, this became a wonder to some in the dorm. I knew the source, that it was God's power of immunity expressed by his spirit the Holy Spirit. This was my first experience with God in this dimension, and I loved it. This is not a difficult process when you realize it is not you but he who does it through you. You need to come to a certain knowledge of God, and after coming to this knowledge, simply activate the faith that knowledge brings. Knowledge indeed brings faith. That whole winter I did not fall sick, and I'm used to catching a cold every winter. If he can do it for a 19-year-old, why can't he do it for you? He is not a respecter of persons, don't starve yourself when there's food in a room next to you, simply because you have not been told. You have now been told, so go in the room and eat the food. Feed your spirit, grow your faith, pray and declare and believe it, and it shall be done in Jesus Name.

Immunity of The Shadow of the almighty:

Now, another way to prevent sickness is to abide under the shadow of he who shall be called Almighty. The bible declares, "He that dwelleth in the secret place of the most high shall abide under the shadow of the Almighty" (Psalms 91:1). Now what is this secret place? What is this shadow? Why is God described as Almighty In this context and not healer? Or savior? And why must we dwell in this secret place to be found abiding under this shadow of which belongs to one called the Almighty? Here's an interpretation. You may describe the word "might", as one's capacity to actualize maximum potential. If one is described as mighty, it means one is exceeding in power. It means he who so ever shall be described as mighty expresses power at near to maximum potential. Now, might can be expressed in different and several contexts. You could say someone is a mighty teacher if he or she teaches with such a great expression that sets them apart from others. You could describe someone as a mighty prayer warrior in the context that he or she can pray powerfully with such great rigor and longevity for hours. You could call the U.S army mighty if they have a reputation for winning most of their wars, and expressing great ease doing it. So, "might" can be expressed in different contexts. And you can be mighty in one area of your life, and not the other. Now, what the bible means by using the word Almighty to describe God is simply this. Of all those that are mighty, he is mightier than they. And in every context of which might may be expressed, he is mighty. So, in simpler terms, God is mighty in every context 1, and any who display might in any context is no match for the might of God. Now, the word shadow is used in this verse to display the issue of protection. It is there to emphasize the point of prevention. Whenever you're under something, you're likely to be protected by it. When it rains, you often use umbrellas, and you hide under the umbrella to protect you from the rain. What the bible is saying here is simply, If you dwell in the secret place, you will be protected from any and everything both mighty and not, in every and any context because you are protected by one who is mightier than all and in every context. So, if the devil is presumed mighty, because he does not bear the description of Almighty, he will be defeated by one who bears that description. God is the only one who bears that description, so it means who so ever decides to dwell in the secret place shall have nothing to worry because they are protected from everything in every area including sickness. So, what is this secret place? The secret place is simply your time in the presence of God. Your time alone with God. The word secret in that verse is there to emphasize the point of privacy and alone time with God without distraction. Your personal time with God, in which you leave everything and spend time with God somewhere. So why must we dwell here in order to abide under the protection of he who is Almighty? A dwelling is a place of shelter, a place of feeding, a place of retreat, a place that brings comfort, a place of relaxation, a place of rest. It is a place where great time is spent. So, when we dwell in this secret place, we will abide, meaning to accept his protection by walking in obedience to his rules by the act of free will through understanding and knowledge. So, dwelling in the presence of God, will cause certain things to happen in our lives causing us to live under his authority which automatically gains us security and protection from him concerning all areas we are able to receive. What this verse is simply saying is if you make God your dwelling place, you will get to a point in which you will want to do all that is necessary to remain under the protection of God, and one of the many advantages of being under the protection of God is protection against sickness.

❖ Create Time. You see, in order to become immune to something, time is needed. The word "dwell" indicates familiarity by the consistency of frequency. In other words, to dwell somewhere means you have become familiar with that place by the numerous times you've visited or inhabited a particular place. Now, knowing that the secret place is your private time with God, the first step is to have a time set. You have a time for work I suppose, a time for school, a time for sleep, a time to celebrate a birthday, a time to have lunch, to have a wedding, to propose, etc... So, create time for God. You can proceed by giving God 30 minutes of your day, and as you progress In consistency you will increase in capacity, this means after some time you may increase your time with God to 1 hour, and so forth. So the first thing you need to do at this moment if you don't have a time set for God every day is to finish reading this paragraph, and decide on a time you want to give God based on your daily schedule, and when you do that, you may continue reading.

❖ Have a place to spend time with God. The house of God is not enough. The house of God(church) is for collaborative fellowship with other children of God. You need personal time with God. The word "secret" in secret place is there to also emphasize privacy and alone time with God. You need to find a place you go to spend time with God. It can be anywhere right, as long as you consistently spend time with God there, it doesn't mean you can't spend time with God in other places, but remember the word of God makes mention of the "secret place" not the "secret places", so it is ideal that you have a particular place where you will consistently spend time with God privately, this will be known as the secret place for you. So again, after reading this paragraph, please decide on a place you will like to spend with God in, and make sure it's a place you will have privacy for you and God alone. Now after finding a place to spend time with God, what do you do? You have fellowship with God in the secret place. You talk to God here. Tell him about your issues, your concerns, ask him how he's doing. God wants a relationship with you. Talk to him, he may not reply in the beginning, but just keep talking to him, in time he may respond back. This is a matter of consistency and faith, and there are many examples in the bible of God responding to consistency and faith. So, prayer takes place in the secret place, and not just about yourself but about others as well as the will of God. Worship also takes place here. Make this place a place of worship. You can worship God in many ways, through musical songs, through thanksgiving, and many others, so as long as you're worshiping, you're making effective use of the secret place. The secret place is a place of edifying your spirit through the word. Reading the bible here is also a good start. Do whatsoever you're led by God to do in the secret place, because there are times God may want to give you specific instructions, and he may wait till you go to the secret place before he makes it known to you. This is a place God will speak to you, so the more consistent you are in your visitation to this place for the purpose of fellowship with God, the better.

❖ Make the secret place a dwelling place. We all allow the occurrence of certain events to take place at certain times, but at the end of all those events, we return back to a place we call "home". Likewise, if you have any issues, troubles, news, events of joy, and everything else that affects your life, make it a habit to share these things with God, and specifically share them in the secret place. At the end of your day at work, or school, or before school or work, whatever time you set as your time to spend with God alone, make sure to bring these things up with God. God wants to hear about your day, the good things he's done for you and about the issues the devil's bombarding you with. Spend so much time in the secret place you become accustomed to it. As normal as brushing your teeth is, spending your selected time in your selected place with God must become normal as well. Doing this consistently will make the secret place a dwelling place. You know the secret place has become a dwelling place when you can't wait to go there and spend time with God every day. You know the secret place has become a dwelling place when it is a place of spiritual exercise for you, a place of spiritual empowerment, a place to build your relationship with God, a place of rest for you in terms of all the noise going on In the world. You know the secret place has become a dwelling place when you begin to abide under the shadow of the Almighty.

❖ Abiding under the shadow of the almighty. Abiding under the shadow of the almighty is guaranteed to happen after truly dwelling in the secret place of the most high. To abide under the shadow of the almighty is simply to find rest in God. It means to walk in the council of God. It means to do whatever you can to stay under the shadow of God, under his protection, it means God is your leader, and you follow him and his ways. To abide under the shadow means to invest into God's protection by accepting his rulership, and Lordship over your life, and in doing so, no one mighty or not will be able to have you because the almighty is your shield, and your protector. One of the signs of one who truly abides under the secret place is when the love of righteous begins to emerge. One who is slow to sin and quick to repentance is one who has made the secret place a dwelling place and therefore now abides under the shadow of he who is Almighty. You will notice many things will begin to run from you once you begin to abide under the shadow of the almighty, one of which is sickness.

❖ Protection from Sickness. We must come to the understanding that sickness is one of the many benefits of abiding under the shadow of the Almighty. There isn't anything special you must do, as long as you dwell in the secret place, you will abide under the shadow, and once you begin to abide, sickness will no longer be a problem. Again, truly abiding is staying away from sin, and living in righteousness. Don't begin to dwell in the secret place for the sole purpose of avoiding sickness, there are many benefits to abiding, and your goal for dwelling in order to abide should be Love. Let your love for God sponsor your desire to dwell in the secret place, therefore allowing you to abide under his shadow, because to they that love God, all things will work together for their good (Romans, 8:28).

Antidote:

Now, just in case you get sick, and you'd like to receive divine healing (non-natural healing), you can access the healing power of Jesus. Now medicine is definitely good for treating sickness, and this book is in no way disregarding or discrediting the benefit of medicine, but we will be focusing on non-natural/medicine-based healing and rather on the divine healing power of Jesus. At some point in time, you may have gotten sick, and some of you may be sick at this time, I pray through this book, you are able to receive your healing in Jesus Name. Now there are different types of sickness and different levels of them, affecting different areas of the body, some appearing to be permanent, and some temporary, some inherited and some attracted. But all these things are no match for the healing power of Jesus Christ. Now we need to know why we are able to be healed. Sickness came into being when Man fell into sin. You when man sinned, it brought death, and so anything that could cause mankind to die was legally allowed to harass the life of man, one of which was sickness. So, the first you should know is if you've been sick and have not died, give glory to God, because the devil brings sickness to kill, so the fact that you haven't died is an act of the sovereign mercy of Elohim, so take some time now to give him glory, for you're not reading this book by accident neither by coincidence, it is my belief that God wanted you to read this, and that is why you are. Now, after Jesus came to die for our sins, he put sickness to death as well, and our job is to access that healing he has for us in order to put sickness in its rightful place, death. Now, there are several ways to access the divine healing power of Christ Jesus our Lord.

Antidote of Faith:

Now, when it comes to the topic of Faith, there is much to say, being that the Lord has put me through many trials and events to get my Faith to a certain level enough to bring forth certain dimensions of his power. In this context, we'll talk about how to apply faith to cure an illness, whether it's a headache, fever, cold, etc... Faith in Jesus Christ can unlock and siphon the power of the Holy Spirit towards the manifestation of healing. Please note that Faith is not the power that brings forth the manifestation, Faith only activates the power to function. Now, faith healing is not reserved for Men and Women of God only, it is accessible by all who believe in the name of Jesus. For it is written in Mark 16:17-18; "And these sings shall follow them that believe; in my name they shall cast out devils; they shall speak in new tongues; They shall take up serpents; and if they drink any deadly thing, it shall not hurt them; **they shall lay hands on the sick, and they shall recover**". Did you know that some illnesses and diseases have no rooted natural causes but rather rooted unnatural causes? In other words, some illnesses are caused by spirits and demonic forces. And Jesus said in the verse above that if we believe, we shall cast out devils. Some of these devils are the causes of many sicknesses and illnesses, and Jesus has given us the power to cast them out. There are also some sicknesses that have natural causes, and Jesus said in the verse above, that if we believe, we can lay hands on the sick and they shall recover, this includes you as well. You have the power to lay hands on yourself if you're sick, and you'll recover. Now, before we can begin to teach you how to activate the healing power of God through faith, there's something we need understand. When it comes to healing, because sickness can have both a natural cause and a supernatural cause, you may need discernment to know what the cause is, in order to appropriately tackle it. But if you have not developed your discernment enough to discern what the cause of a particular sickness is, here are some signs to help you discern.

Signs of the involvement of a spirit(demons) in sickness;

(Please note: coming into the actualization of these signs does not make it a definite conclusion that spirits are involved, but it does indeed indicate of such possibilities.)

-The doctors find nothing wrong physically

-The doctors can't pinpoint a particular cause

-The sickness is unnatural, it's different, it is rare or unseen before

-The sickness runs in the family, from generation to generation (Hereditary)

-You suddenly had a dream where you ate in it, and sickness followed shortly after

Now, of course, not every sickness is caused by a spirit, there are some that have natural causes, but the reason you'll want to know which ones are caused by spirits and which ones are not is because if you attempt to cure a sickness with faith, or by medicine, and it is a sickness caused by spirits, then your efforts may either not amount to much, or it may take care of the symptoms but illness will still be there, and therefore the symptoms may be temporarily gone, but they may return until you deal with the root cause. Now, let's discuss how to access the healing power of God through faith.

❖ Grow in Faith. It is written that Faith comes by hearing and hearing by the word of God (Romans 10:17). So, faith comes by knowledge. Because hearing is one of the ways we acquire knowledge, and the word of God is a form of knowledge. It's God's knowledge. The word of God is God himself in word formation. So, Faith comes by hearing knowledge. And it is that knowledge that sponsors your faith, and it is faith that sponsors your works for a manifestation. So, in order to get the manifestation of healing, sponsored by Faith, we must go back to what sponsors your faith, and how strong it is. The word of God should be the only sponsor of your faith. This means, you must begin to hear things you want to apply your faith to. So, if you want to apply your faith to sickness, you must hear things about healing. Read the word of God. Listen to messages about the word of God. Since it is healing we are talking about, read healings scriptures. Listen to messages about the healing power of Christ Jesus. This is because what you hear will build your faith, allowing your faith to grow, and when you have a sufficient supply of it, you'll be able to apply it to sickness, therefore causing the healing power of Christ to remove sickness from your life. So, what you need to do is to reduce your hearing and seeing of things that do not help you grow in faith. Because since faith in God cometh by hearing and hearing by the word, Faith in medicine and natural cures also comes by hearing and hearing by television media, social media, etc... So, you will need to stop building your faith in Man's cure and start building your faith in God's cure. Now, of course there's nothing wrong with taking medicine or using man's cure to illness, but this is a book about Kingdom dimensions, and this is the subject of healing, so this book will teach divine healing on this earth. So, grow your faith in Jesus Christ and his healing power by reading scriptures about healing, listening to messages about healing, and pray to God to heal you. Now, if you're more persistent, and would like to speed up the process, you may want to fast. Fasting is one of the fastest ways to increase your faith by allowing your spirit to have more dominance and control over your body and what you do. Another way to speed up the process is to pray in the spirit (for those who can) for at least 1hour daily for some months (you choose). Do this consecutively. Read the bible (you can focus on healing scriptures), then pray in the spirit(for those who can), if you can't pray in the spirit, pray in your understanding(your language), tell God to increase your faith in prayer, to allow you to lay hands and the sick will recover, and fast if you can, you can start from 8am -12pm as a beginner and don't eat or watch any cellular shows or tv, just pray and read the word of God during your fasting time, you may listen to sermons, and you can focus on healing during your fast. Doing these things frequently and consistently will help you grow and get to a place of maturity. Surround yourself with people who believe in the healing power of God, you may need to cut some friends off if you truly want to grow in faith, in order to have the supply of faith that can bring manifestations of healing. You must make certain sacrifices to host the supernatural power of God. Acting like everybody will get you the results of everybody but spending with God will get you the God kind of results.

❖ Mature in Faith (Trust). I have come to the understanding that Trust is the Maturity of Faith. The moment you trust someone, your faith in them has been matured, it is prime. This is what trusting God and his word means. You must mature your faith in him, mature your faith in his word. Maturity is only obtained out of consistent growth. It is very important that your faith in God is matured, earning you the status of one who fully Trusts in him. It is when you do this, that you can effectively quench doubt, and allow Faith to activate the healing power of Christ. You need to get your faith to a level where you trust God (it is no longer a hope, but a realm where you have no other option but him). If you're sick and you lay hands on the area of illness, and pray to be healed, do you trust that God will heal you? This is a good place to start. So, if you've put into practice the things written above in the (grow in faith) section, you should grow in faith. Now, you don't necessarily have to be perfectly mature in faith before you can start to see results. You just need to believe he can heal you through yourself for this to work. Just trust God.

❖ Begin to lay hands on the sick. Now, it doesn't matter whether you're fully mature or not, as long as you're at basic/minimum maturity, meaning as long as you trust God enough to believe he can heal others and yourself through your hands, then you're ready to minister the healing power of our Lord. Now let us start with ministering healing to yourself. I'm speaking from experience, before I started ministering healing to others, I began with myself, and The Lord took me through several processes. The Holy Spirit taught me these things as I had no teacher to teach me, but by the grace of Elohim, he sent me out with a mission to teach and mature the body of Christ as I'm doing now by writing this book. Let's start with minor sickness (headaches, pains, hiccups, etc). My very first actualized encounter with healing was when I was lying down on the bed in my dorm room freshman year. I had been doing the things I wrote about above for you to do in order to grow your faith. This particular day I don't remember doing anything special. I was laying on my bed, and I got a hiccup. And I don't know why I did this, but I took my hand, and put my two fingers (index and middle) on my throat, and I spoke these words; "Be Gone". And behold, the hiccups left(instantly). This was my first realized encounter with God's healing power, and since then, anytime someone has a hiccup, I would also go to them and ask if I could pray for them, then I would do the same thing. I would lay hands on their throat and say, "Be Gone", and behold it will always go 100% of the time(instantly). Now of course the Holy Spirit trained me in expelling sicknesses I would call more "serious", and I will write of another testimony in the next few pages to inspire hope and faith. So, what I want you to do is to lay hands on the area of the minor sickness (pain, headaches, hiccups, even fever can be considered minor). Lay hands on that area of sickness, whether it's you or another, and just speak out of the Spirit. Pray for them. Command that spirit of infirmity to go In Jesus Name, and command their body Be healed in Jesus name, and move on. You don't need to check whether it's gone or not, just pray and leave the rest for God. Depending on your faith level, the sickness may either be fully gone immediately, or it may reduce, or nothing may seem to have happened immediately, don't let that stop you, continue building your faith and try again, you'll get to a point where you won't need to speak long, just command the healing, and it will happen instantly.

❖ Personal Testimony. There was a time as I continued to build and grow my faith into full maturity, I caught a flu with symptoms of a high fever, coughing, and sneezing, feeling extremely cold while in fact it was warm in the room, I was heavily sedated with symptoms of a flu. Now, at the time I did not know, but the Lord was using that experience to build my faith. And so I decided, I was not going to take medicine as I previously had been doing when I should encounter things like this. It just so happened that I was praying for at least an hour every day, and that day I did not pray. Now, I'm not saying it was the prayer that kept sickness away, but I'm saying I had grown my spirit, and grown in faith to a certain maturity by frequent and quantitative prayer, and God used this sickness to test my faith and whether or not I would apply it to cure this flu. So, behold, the flu took hold of my being, and I decided I would not take medicine. I decided to come into the acknowledgement that sickness is not my portion, and that by his stripes we were healed. I looked for healing scriptures to declare, I looked for messages about healing, I tried everything I thought I knew to receive the healing power of Jesus to get rid of this sickness without medicine, until I left everything I was doing, to follow what the Holy Spirit was leading me to do. Take the word of God about healing and believe it. After believing the word of God about healing, I decided not to yield to the sickness. This is the key. This is what the Holy Spirit was teaching me. You see, whatever you yield yourself to, you will express their influence over you. If you yield yourself to alcohol by drinking it, you will express its influence over you. So, I was led by the Holy Spirit not to yield to this sickness, and that was the expression of "works" as a result of the faith I had in God to heal me. You see, when you are sick and you yield to it, it will have influence over you. Now what do I mean by yield? You see, yielding means allowing the power of that sickness to take hold of you. It means you agree that you should be sick, it means you're accepting that sickness, you agree that sickness has power of you, and therefore you let it run its course. To get rid of sickness, you must begin by failing to yield to it. You must know, believe, and trust that God's word is truth, and that sickness has no power of over you anymore in Christ. So, when you start feeling symptoms of sickness, try not to yield to it. Try your best to do things you would normally do as if the sickness wasn't present (of course, things that would not put you in any more harm. Also please note, do not do this if it will harm you further, especially if your faith has not grown large enough to accommodate such practices. I advise practicing on less-serious issues like coughs or headaches but if you feel medicine is the best solution, please take it. This may not be for everybody, but for the few that are chosen to unlock the healing power of Christ through this route). Declare the word of God, "Sickness you have no power of me". Then, lay hands on yourself, and say "Thou spirit of infirmity, Be Gone in Jesus Name, I cast you out now, leave my body now In Jesus Name". Then say this after, "Be healed in Jesus name", speak the name of whatever sickness is oppressing you, and say "Be gone, and body Be healed now In Jesus name". Now if you're just beginning you will most likely notice that you may still sense the symptoms, don't let that affect your faith, just believe that the declarations of healing you pronounced over your body is taking effect, and continue to do what you need to do. Now after I decided not to yield to the influence of the sickness, things did not instantly change. Now, at that time I believe I was around the age of 19, and when I decided not to yield to the sickness despite the growing influence of the symptoms, I could hear the voice of demons speaking in my ears, telling me to go and take medicine, that there is no faith, that I will sleep and wake up and I will still be sick and that I won't be able to make it to church the next day and I will disappoint the choir, because at that time I was in the choir as the pianist, and so we rehearsed on that Saturday I caught the flu, and the next day was Sunday, and it was a Christmas service so I was really needed because the songs were piano dependent. So, the devil used my reluctance to disappoint the church and the choir and my duty as pianist to try to manipulate me to deport my efforts in the actualization of the appliance of faith in the expression of healing. But behold, I ignored that voice, and I covered myself with blankets because I was cold even though it was warm. I decided I will not allow the loud symptoms of this sickness to rob me of my Faith in the immortal healer, The Lord God. So, I held on to my faith, and I believed that by the next day when I wake up, the sickness will be gone, or at least it will reduce. So, I slept that night with all those symptoms. And behold, this was the first time I got to see what actually goes on in the spirit when you refuse to yield to sickness by faith even though you feel all the symptoms live and very strongly. I had a dream that night, and behold I was in the spirit realm, and I saw my spirit wrestling with another spirit of whom I was made aware that it was the spirit of infirmity that had taking hold of my body, the spirit responsible for causing the symptoms I was feeling. Now in the spirit, I was on one opposite side, and the spirit was on the opposite side, and there was something in between us. Now the interesting thing about this was I knew exactly what was going on. You see in the spirit; I and this infirmity were going back and forth like a tag of war. For those of you who don't know what tag of war is, it is when one or more persons are on one side and one or more persons are on the other side and there's a rope in between them, and there's a line right in the middle of both of them, and the goal is to pull the other person(s) on the other side in order to get them to cross that line in the middle. This was what was happening with me and that spirit in the spiritual realm. So, I could see that my spirit was in a tag of war-type scenario with this spirit of infirmity, and I knew (not sure how) but I knew that it was faith I was using to wrestle with this spirit, Faith was my strength, and behold I woke up. And the Holy Ghost told me to pray in tongues (praying in the spirit), and I did. And after about 30 minutes or so, I fell asleep, and I woke up. And behold, when I awoke, the symptoms had died down, I was about 60% healed. And by the night, I was completely healed, no medicine, no treatment, just Faith in the healing power of Christ Jesus our Lord. Now, since then I hadn't gotten any fever, flu, cough, or any of those symptoms again for about 2 years, till a time I was outside in the cold without proper covering, and I stayed in that cold for almost an hour, and behold, I felt my throat feeling like it was developing a cough, and I felt my body beginning to feel like it wants to develop a fever. Now remember it's been 2 years without contracting this sickness, and of course at this time, I'd grown in Christ and in Faith. So, when I stayed in the cold for almost an hour and begun to feel these symptoms, Immediately I rebuked that spirit instantly and laid hands on my throat and commanded it to be well and behold, within a matter of minutes, it was gone. Have you noticed the difference between what happened two years earlier and two years later? Two years earlier, the sickness was able to manifest itself at full potential, and it took about a day for recovery without medical treatment. Now two years later, the infirmity was cast out before it could even have time to get comfortable in my body, and the symptoms left withing minutes. This is growth. You will start without immediate change, but as you grow in Christ, you will grow into maturity bringing forth immediate healing. I have many more testimonies about healing, especially with much more serious illnesses including one of my largest testimonies which involves an incurable birth condition I was completely healed from. Now, there are also testimonies about the healing of others. My very first serious "healing/miracle" on someone else was a lady who had a broken/injured leg and was given a leg brace as well pain medication for the pain she'd been having. At this time, I was part of various campus bible studies. And I met this young lady at one of the bible studies. So, she came into the bible study limping with her leg brace on, and bible study went on as normal. But after bible study was over, and prayer points where being raised for those who needed prayer for specific things, people began to make their prayer points known and the young lady was part of them. She mentioned that her leg had been injured for a while, and nothing was working. She was still in pain and her leg was still not healed after the medication and the brace. So, she mentioned that the group should pray that God will heal her. Now after the bible study was over, I was on my way out when I saw the young lady attempting to walk out, and immediately I felt convicted by the Holy Ghost to pray for her leg. I knew God had sent me there to minister healing to her as it was her prayer point to God. So, I walked to her, and asked if I could pray for her leg. She said sure (with a tone that seemed like she did not believe anything would happen but she was open to prayer). So, I kneeled, and laid hands on the leg and prayed by commanding the leg to "be healed", and the pain to "be gone" in Jesus name. And that was it. I got up and left. And at a later bible study, she had no brace on her leg, and told me her testimony, and later mentioned it to the bible study group. She mentioned that from the moment I prayed for her, to the moment she reached her dorm, her leg was completely healed, and the pain had left. I was amazed that God would do this because I had been used to doing this with my own body but to minister healing to another person and the person would get healed, especially from something that wasn't a hiccup was quite amazing. I did not expect the healing to be much neither did I expect it to be fast, but the Lord did it. This was my first major healing testimony from someone else. The reason I included this was to make this point. You're learning to access the healing power of Christ and that's good. But it's not just meant for you, but for others. The healing power I had seen in my own body had now begun to flow on others by simply applying Mark 16:17-18, just lay hands on the sick, and the rest will be left to God to recover them. So, as you practice healing on yourself, you may ask to pray for people, and you'll be surprised to see them recover. Some may ask, "but it is written, some where given the gifts of healing, what if I don't have it?" Please note that this has to do with your calling/ministry. There is something called a healing anointing, and there is something called the possession of every believer. Every believer has the power to lay hands on the sick, and they will recover (Mark 16:17-18). The contingency with this type of recovery is that you have to believe. As long as you believe, recovery will take place (contingent on God's ability to exercise his sovereignty to prevent recovery for any reason). Now please note, the bible mentions, "they will recover". The word recovery indicates a process. It allows time to be the administrator of the recovery. So, in other words, when you lay hands on the sick to exercise your rights as a believer, healing will take place (contingent on the sovereignty of God) but it will be a recovery process, meaning it will take time. Now, when it comes to the gifts of healing towards the physical body, there is an anointing in assistance. So usually, when you operate with the gifts of healing towards body sickness, you will feel an anointing on you. Most people feel heat on their hands, or something like electricity on their hands. Some will feel it on their heads, others will feel it elsewhere depending on their personal calling and walk with God. When it comes to the healing anointing, I feel it on the right side of my face. It feels like steam without heat. When I feel this, no contact is necessary (for most illnesses), and healing is usually instant. For the sake of the general population, we won't talk about the healing anointing but rather the power available to every believer in Christ. So please, you don't need to have a gift of healing to minister healing, you just need to lay hands and believe as the word of God states. Make sure to practice what you've learned, and when you feel confident and have grown in faith, with their consent, you may begin to pray for people as you're led by God.

The Cure

Fear

—

Recipients:

This represents the specific entity of our being that may be affected by the problem of fear.

|| Spirit - **Soul** - Body

Area of Focus:

This represents the specific entity we will focus on providing the antidote to as well as the immunity to prevent.

❖ || The Fear of the Soul

Category:

Place, Operation, Companionship, Satisfaction

Antidote:

Now in the realm of fear, there are quite a few expressions and categories of the operations of this power. For the purpose of the context of this book, we will discuss the type of fear that is ungodly, the fear that is the product of the spirit of fear, of which it was written, did not come from God (2 Timothy 1:7). Everybody, at some point has been afraid of something. Before we can

—

begin to discuss about immunities and antidotes of fear, we must go to the beginning to find out where fear came from, and what caused it, then we can progress to finding a solution both a preventive one and a repellant one. It is written, "He answered, "I heard you in the garden, and I was afraid because I was naked; so I hid (Genesis 3:10). This is Adam's response to God after sinning. So, the first thing Adam did after committing sin was to hide. And that action of hiding was the result of a root cause called fear. So that kind of fear was not part of what God wanted man to experience in his original will. That kind of fear came into being after sin intruded the realm of man. Now note, what fear caused Adam and eve to do was to hide. So, one of the actions fear can birth is timidity. So, because Adam and Eve sinned, as opposed to Faith and Boldness in the presence of God, one of the consequences of their sin was a power of fear, which had the ability to do many things, one of which was to cause them to hide from God, whom they previously had fellowship and communion with without fear, but now because of a sinful action, it brought a power that caused them to be ashamed of being in the presence of their maker. Now, because we inherited the sin of our great ancestor Adam, we became liable to the power of fear, but through Jesus Christ our Lord, we are no longer subject to the sin of our ancestors, therefore we are no longer subject to the power of fear. Now, in the realm of Man, there exist a spirit of fear, and unfortunately, some are bound by this spirit, not all but some. Of those that were bound by this spirit, I to was part of them, until Jesus Christ himself liberated me, and I am here to also spread the message of his liberative power to set all free from the power of Fear. Now, when it comes to fear, there is what I call "General Fear" and there's what I call "Spirit aided fear". General fear is what we all have or have had at some point in our life, maybe we were frightened by the sight of an animal that you believe has the ability to harm you. You can also be afraid of anything you feel has the ability to harm you, but the fear is mild, and most likely maybe linked to what you've personally experienced or seen in movies or shows. Another kind of general fear would be if someone startled you by their surprise and unexpected move. All those could be quantified into the general-fear category. But there is a type of fear that is aided by the spirit of fear. Those who are bound by this power will often be afraid beyond natural human measure. For example, people who are very timid may be bound by that spirit. People who have a low self-esteem maybe bound by that spirit. Some other traits that indicate the work of the spirit of fear in a person's life are inclusive but not limited to the following: extreme dislike of attention, the extreme lack of boldness, extreme indecisiveness, the extreme avoidance of confrontation. Again, please note, the expression of these activities in one's life does not make it certain and definite that it is the result of the spirit of fear, but rather most likely, in which I would rate it a 98% chance. Now, fear is so powerful, that it may not only cause one to stay in sin, but it can also cause one to be prevented from boldly executing what God wants to execute, therefore making little to no use of one's life in regard to the will of God, ultimately making that individual's life useless(within eternal context), and when one becomes useless, his or her life no longer has meaning, therefore their time on earth as a result, may be very limited. Again, I to was bound greatly by the spirit of fear, but the Lord on two separate occasions, came to liberate me. One was an encounter where he spoke to me, and explained to me with insight a bit about fear and how it had bound me to certain sins, and another was when he showed me his face as a white flame of fire, both of which took away the spirit of fear in the expressions they had found in my life, and it is also my wish that my experience will allow me to write words sponsored by the Holy Spirit to bring forth the same liberation from fear to you as it was done with me.

Antidote of The Word of God:

Now, as a young child, I would tell lies to get out of trouble with my parents. So, lying became second nature. If I broke something at the house when no one was around, and they came to ask me who did, I would tell them "I don't know" because I did not want to get in trouble. In other words, fear motivated me to lie in order to prevent trouble. I was afraid of trouble, so I lied. Now, as I grew up, fear had more and more of a hold on me, that I became very timid. I would be afraid of people because I did not want to get in trouble with them. I would be afraid of telling people the truth because I did not want to hurt their feelings. I avoided doing certain things in front of certain people because I was afraid of what they'd think. So, the spirit of fear held me bound so much that I became indecisive. I was afraid to make the wrong choice so I couldn't choose. So, when God decided he was going to use me, he called me into a fast. So, I began to fast and pray. That was my very first long fasting and praying session, and it was for 30 days, as I was led by the Holy Spirit to fast. Now, during this 30 day fast I had a few encounters, one of which was that God spoke to me very clearly about many things, but one of which was about fear. You see, God had chosen to use me, so he knew that he can't effectively use someone who is bound by the spirit of fear, so he had to address that. During this fast, on one of the days, the Lord began to speak to me about fear. Note that, this is the first time I'm hearing God clearly, and acknowledging it. He said, "Stop Lying", "Be bold". He said, "Be decisive". Then he told me the reason I would lie/exaggerate or refrain from telling the truth is because of fear. He told me the reason I was indecisive was because of fear. Then he said this, and this is what got me to change my ways, not the fact that he told me to stop, but because of this. This is what got me to be free and bold enough to tell the truth. He said, "Fear not man, for he did not create you". Wow, when I heard this, I was

70

liberated. In other words, he's saying, no man is worth being on the receiving end of your fear. He is saying, if at all one must fear, it should be him and him alone, and no one else. Man is not in charge of his/her life. Man can fall sick tomorrow, man can die tomorrow, man is mortal, so why fear one who is formed out of dust? Just think about it. Any form of lying is the result of fear. Fear is the root cause of lying, insecurities, indecisiveness, etc... Imagine something happened at work, and you lie about it because you're afraid you'll get fired. Is God not in charge of the heart of your boss? Why lie because you're afraid man will fire you. Can't that individual fall sick? Can't they be relocated? Aren't they mortal enough to accommodate death? So why are you afraid. Hear me and hear me well, "Fear not man, for he did not create you". That's the word of the Lord to you. I believe it was not just for me but for all those bound by the spirit of fear, I pray you receive your liberation in the name of Jesus. After God had spoken this word to me, he reassured me to his written word. He gave me a bible verse. Again, this was the first time I had received a bible verse from the Spirit of God. It just appeared in my mind like a thought, but I had not even read this in the bible before, so it was a confirmation when I read it, after he had just spoke to me about fear. He gave me the verse 2 Timothy 1:7, which sates "For God has not given us the spirit of fear, but of power, and of love, and of a sound mind". So, fear alone can prevent the expression of power, it can restrict love, and it can take away sound mind. So, because of this encounter with God, the sins I committed with links to fear were abolished. It took time for me, and I may take time for you as well, but I pray that by the power of the word of God, written or spoken, you are free from the spirit of fear in Jesus name. So, speak this word over your life. And whenever you are about to lie, remember the words "fear not man, for he did not create you". Whenever you are about to commit any sin that has roots to fear, remember those words, and remember 2 Timothy 1:7, and speak those words over your life, and resist that spirit, until it is expelled by the power of Jesus.

Antidote of an encounter:

Now, another way to be set free from fear is by an encounter. Now, an encounter may set you free from a different kind of expression of fear. The first type of fear we discussed previously was a fear that sponsored certain kinds of sins like lying. But this kind of fear does necessarily sponsor certain actions of sin, but rather exposes one to the ideology of being unprotected, therefore causing one to panic out of fear. So being afraid of the dark because one feels as if there are demons waiting to attack them, so such individuals may sleep with the lights on. Another example would be being afraid to drive on bridges or take airplanes because they are afraid it is very unsafe, so therefore Individuals of that ideologies may refrain from using planes as a mode of transportation or driving over bridges as a path to their destinations. This kind of fear is quite strong and can cause one to be restricted in experience. And it can strongly derive its power out of ignorance. A biblical example of this type of fear would be in 2 kings 13:6-20, when the king wanted to capture the prophet Elisha, and the king sent an army to capture him, and the servant looked and saw the army of the king, and the servant was afraid and said to Elisha in verse 15, "Oh no, my lord! What shall we do?" the servant asked". Then Elisha replied him in verse 16 and 17, "Don't be afraid," the prophet answered. "Those who are with us are more than those who are with them." And Elisha prayed, "Open his eyes, LORD, so that he may see." Then the LORD opened the servant's eyes, and he looked and saw the hills full of horses and chariots of fire all around Elisha". So, this type of fear can be derived out of ignorance. The servant reacted based on what he saw physically, but spiritually, they were protected, and since the spiritual realm rules the physical, all Elisha had to do was asked God to strike them with blindness, and they became blind, and he led them elsewhere. So, this is the type of fear I'm referring to, a fear that brings faithlessness, a fear that encourages doubt and distrust in God. A fear that magnifies the devil and minimizes God. It is unhealthy to have this kind of fear, and one way to overcome the spirit of fear in this regard is through an encounter. God is the one in charge of encounters. It is through his sovereignty that encounters are issued out. Now even if you have not had an encounter, you can still benefit from another's encounter. I want to share mine with you, and I hope that this will get you to have faith in God, believing that he does protect you, even if it seems you are physically alone. Now after God had rescued me from the fear that caused me to commit certain sins as a young child, there was still fear in my heart towards other things. One of which was the fear of demons and other entities of the enemy that God has given us power over. There was a night, I don't remember doing anything special. I was asleep, alone in the room, of course with the lights off, and a blanket over me on the couch. Then behold, I found myself having a very frightening dream. I awoke from that dream the most frightened I had ever been before in my entire life. I woke up shaking, gasping for air, and so because of the heavy intensity of fear I woke up with as a result of such a dream that I have not forgotten to this day, I was afraid to open my eyes, so I kept them closed, and cuddled up and kept the blanket over me, and I remained on that couch with extreme fear. I thought if I opened my eyes, I would see demons in the room considering the dream I just had. So, I kept my eyes close, and head tucked in. Note, this is not a nightmare. We've all had nightmares at some point, yes, they can cause fear, but this was different. This dream was no ordinary dream, neither was it a nightmare, but a revelational dream. Now because of the extensity of fear I was feeling, I was so afraid to get up, but too afraid to go back to bed because I did not want to dream again, so I was in a state of perplexity. I was too overwhelmed with fear to do anything, and behold, at once, I saw the face of Jesus Christ as a white flame of fire. He projected his face to me as my eyes were closed. This was not a vision, neither was it in person, I could see his face with the eye of my spirit. His eyes looked like white flames of fire, his hair was like a white flame of fire, his entire face appeared to me as a white flame of fire. He did not speak, I only saw him, looking at me, and I he. As I began to see this, I noticed that the fear I had begun to dwindle down, it began to reduce. Now, I cannot tell how long it was that I saw his face, but I realized after some time, I was no longer afraid, and so I sat up from the couch, I could still see his face, but it began to reduce in intensity of light, like someone was turning up the opacity. It did not matter whether my eyes were closed or opened, I could still see his face, whether I turned left or right, I could still see his face. It was as if he projected his face as a white flame of fire to me in between the spiritual and physical. Then after some time, his face slowly disappeared, and I saw him no more that night/dawn. After his face had gone, it was as if I had no fear. I was completely bold. The lights were still off, I was still alone, and yet no fear. In fact, I got up to get my phone to look up if they had the real face of Jesus on the internet, or at least the face I saw. I found it. Then I went to sleep after that in peace. And since then, my tolerance for fear has reduced. It's like someone had took a nob of fear in my heart and turned it down. Just seeing the face of our Lord, caused my fear to be greatly reduced, and at that time, it was like I had no fear whatsoever. Now, though there was no speaking involved here, the message was quite clear. God wanted to show me that I had nothing to fear. All I had to do was to look upon him, and I would be safe. All I had to do was to find security in him. He was making the point that there is no being that is greater than he, therefore, as long as he is on our side, we are safe. He was simply trying to say, "I'm here son". This was how Jesus comforted me in the midst of my greatest experience of fear, and as a result, never again will I experience that kind of fear, and I pray the same for you in Jesus name. Now, I told you that story to impart a certain revelation to your spirit. We are often afraid of things because we do not see them how God sees them, we only see them how man sees them. No demon could do me any harm because God was with me, but I could not see it, so I was afraid, but Jesus showed me that he was with me and that took the fear away. Elisha's servant was afraid of the king's troops because he could not see what Elisha saw. When his eyes were opened, he was no longer afraid. You see we're afraid because we can't see, but once we can see, then the fear goes. But we are not always given the chance to see in the spirit, so what God said we should do is to have Faith. He gives us the ability to have faith. And faith is the evidence of things not seen (Hebrews 11:1), so in relation to this context, God is saying, even if I don't open your eyes to see that you are safe and protected in the spirit, I want you to believe it by my word. Is it not written, "But the Lord is faithful, and he will strengthen you and protect you from the evil one" (2 Thessalonians 3:3). So, God is saying, even though you may not be able to see, believe that you are protected, by the assurance of my word, and that faith will be the evidence of your unseen protection. In other words, believing that you are protected on the basis of God's word is comparable to seeing that you are protected in the spirit. So, not everybody may have daily encounters, but you can position yourself to have them. You can't force an encounter, God is sovereign, he does as he pleases, therefore there are no steps or guides into having an encounter with God, but you can position yourself so that you are ready, just in case he wishes to bless you with such. It is wise to maintain an active prayer life, that way you are more perceptive in the spirit. It is also wise to meditate on the word of God frequently. It is also wise to abstain from sinful activities, this will allow you to dive deeper into God with minimal obstacles. At the end of the day, if God feels that an encounter maybe a necessary step in your walk with him, then he may choose to give you encounters unique to your own personal call and work with him, but if it doesn't happen and you're someone who struggles with extreme fear, receive the message of the encounter shared here. You can benefit from it, because the encounter may have been specific ones being(which is I), but the point is general to all. God is indeed with us all, whether we see it or not, so read his word, and believe it, and fear no evil, for indeed he has given us power over all things through Christ by his Spirit, and the sooner you believe it, the faster fear will run away from you.

Immunity:

Now, once you expel fear from your heart, in order to keep that spirit away, you must subscribe to a few things. The hardest part in the school of the removal of fear is indeed packed as the antidote. Once fear is away from your life, you must make sure you stick with Jesus, because it was he who removed it from your life in the first place, so your key to permanent freedom from that spirit is to make sure you're close to Jesus, because only he has the power to truly set you free and keep you free from the enemy.

Immunity of the word:

As long as you consistently declare the word of God's protection over your life, and you believe it, you will remain free. There is nothing stronger than God's word. God's words are not just mere words, but they're life. What God speaks is truth, and the greatest opposition to truth is disbelief. So as long as you are a child of God and you believe in his word, you will see a manifestation in your life, given you have the assistance of the Holy Spirit. So, declare the word of God over your life, confess it over your life, and believe.

Immunity of righteousness:

Now there are some mechanics to certain things in the Kingdom. Given the contexts of certain topics expounded in this book, it is not given that I should deploy certain knowledge about certain things though I have been given access, but for the sake of efficiency, I will only explain what is needed. You see, the devil's end goal in life is to take your soul with him to were he's going. The only way he can do that, is to cause you to sin and rebel against God. Now, if he can't win your soul because you've given your life to Jesus, then he will try to make you suffer while you're on earth, in order to prevent you from fulfilling the plan of God for your life. So even though your eternal life is secured in Christ, your eternal relevance and ordination may be hindered from full expression. In other words, if he can't still your eternal life, he can still steal your eternal reward(s) if you let him. You see, the devil knows that God has supplied us grace by the Spirit of God to live a righteous life, and as long as we live a righteous life, and do his will, we are in good terms with God. So, in order for the devil to bring misery to a child of God, he needs to do it legally, so he must first create a situation that cause us to sin, then when we sin, he then has a legal entry point to bring forth disaster, especially if we don't repent from those sins. So, active sinning without repentance can allow the devil to issue back the spirit of fear into your life. Remember it was sin that caused fear to run and attach itself to the heart of Adam and Eve, causing them to hide from God. So, to maintain freedom from the spirit of fear, make sure to avoid sin as much as you can, and if you do fall, then get back up by repenting from that/those sin(s) and seek forgiveness.

Unforgiveness

Recipients:

This represents the specific entity of our being that may be affected by the problem of unforgiveness.

|| Spirit - **Soul** - Body

Area of Focus:

This represents the specific entity we will focus on providing the antidote to as well as the immunity to prevent.

|| Unforgiveness of the Soul

Category:

Satisfaction

Antidote:

Unforgiveness is quite an easy behavior to fall into, but it has a serious eternal implication. Many may come to find that it may not be murder that gets people away from eternal life, neither lying nor stealing or adultery nor fornication but rather unforgiveness. This is because those sins can be seen physically, and so you can repent from them and ask God to forgive you and never do them again. But when it comes to unforgiveness, it is of the

---

heart, and so it can often be neglected, and not counted as anything serious. But unforgiveness is so dangerous that it can prevent our sins from being forgiven. Now, in order to be free from the binding power of unforgiveness, we need to go to the roots, to understand how it is birthed and matured, in order to execute an appropriate antidote to expel it from our hearts. Now, it is written, "In your anger do not sin: Do not let the sun go down while you are still angry" (Ephesians 4:26). So, the first thing to note here is that there are two variations of anger here. Active anger, and inactive anger. So, the first part of this scripture commands us not to sin in anger. This refers to the sinful actions anger can birth. Some of these actions include fights, degrading insults, etc... So certain actions of sin are more likely to occur under the influence of the perceptive view of anger. So, anger in itself is not a sin (God gets angry), it is simply an exhaustion of your tolerance. It is when you allow this exhaustion of tolerance to compel you to commit an unrighteous action that you have entered into the realms of sin. All this is still the active portion of anger. The inactive portion of anger is what leads to unforgiveness. So, the second part of the scripture instructs us not to allow the sun to go down on our anger. This is the inactive portion of anger, and when anger is still in existence after a while, it gives birth to unforgiveness. Now why do you think it says don't let the sun go down on your anger? Well, to answer that we need to take a look at this scripture. It is written, "And there was evening, and there was morning, the first day" (Genesis 1:5). So, we know here that evening starts out the day, and morning comes to end it. We also know that the sun is the sign that alerts us that morning has begun. So, when the sun goes down, it is a sign that the day is ending, and the new day is beginning. So, in other words, according to biblical terminology, the day ends when the sun goes down, and a new day begins when evening starts. So, what Ephesians 4:26 declares when we are instructed not to allow the sun to go down in our anger is that we

80

should not allow the day to end while we are angry, we should not allow the new day to begin with us angry. So, we may think we are not committing a sin by holding anger in, as long as we do not commit certain actions, but holding that anger in for long enough will cause unforgiveness to be born. So, the moment you've been given a chance to let go of your anger, and you don't, unforgiveness has been born. And the moment you let unforgiveness settle in your heart, it becomes mature, and when it is mature, it is much more difficult to overcome, but not impossible. Now here's what unforgiveness really does concerning our eternal destination. It is written, "After this manner therefore pray ye: Our Father which art in heaven, Hallowed be thy name. Thy kingdom come, Thy will be done in earth, as it is in heaven. Give us this day our daily bread. And forgive us our debts, as we forgive our debtors. And lead us not into temptation but deliver us from evil: For thine is the kingdom, and the power, and the glory, forever. Amen. For if ye forgive men their trespasses, your heavenly Father will also forgive you: But if ye forgive not men their trespasses, neither will your Father forgive your trespasses" (Mathew 6:9-15). We see here that when Jesus was teaching his disciples how to pray (this applies to us also), he made mention that God should forgive us our debts as we have forgiven others of their debts/trespasses. These are things we can't pay for, things we owe, for us, this is sin. So, Jesus made it an expectation here that we should already have forgiven others of their debts/trespasses against us before we ask God to forgive our debts/trespasses against him(sin). Now, it is written, "Or do you not know, that the unrighteous will not inherit the kingdom of God?" (1 Corinthians 6:9). So, we know that sinners who have not been made righteous by the blood of Jesus Christ cannot inherit the Kingdom of God. So, in order for us to be made righteous, our sins must be forgiven. In order for our sins to be forgiven we must ask God to forgive them. Now, we just learned that there is something that can prevent our sins from being forgiven, and that is if we don't forgive others as Jesus stated in the verse 15 of Mathew 9. Now if our sins are not forgiven, it means we've not been made righteous, and if we've not been made righteous it means we are unrighteous, and we read previously that the unrighteous person cannot inherit the kingdom of God, so it means unforgiveness can prevent a person from inheriting the Kingdom of God. This is the true implication of unforgiveness. It is very important that we forgive others, and do it quickly, so that our sins can also be forgiven. Now, here are some practices to help expel unforgiveness from our heart, just in case we have any sin in our lives, after forgiven others, we can ask for forgiveness so that we also may be forgiven, therefore restored to righteousness.

Antidote of communication:

There's one thing God has always wanted with man, and its communication. You see, God made it known to us what he wanted us to do to please him since he's our creator, he created us for a reason, and so it is our job to make sure we fulfill what we were created to do as well as to please God. God created us to have his nature, and so fulfilling his nature of righteousness is pleasing to him. Now, if an individual is unable to secure the spoken will of God, they have the bible to reveal the general will of God. Now, God provided the bible as a guide for those who have not yet mastered their communication skills with God to know what he wants for us. So, God made his general will accessible through his written word. You see, God found a way to communicate his will to us, even to those who are not quite familiar with hearing his voice yet. This is here to highlight the importance of communication. In order to do, you must know. You can't efficiently perform an action without direct or indirect knowledge. So, God made sure to communicate what he expected out of the creation of Man in some way, in order for man to know how to please him, and therefore man could now choose, out of their will to do so. Now, when we sin, God expects us to communicate to him by asking for forgiveness, doing so will allow him to cleanse us from our impurities. How could God cleanse us if we don't ask by communication? Is it not written that "ye have not because ye ask not" (James 4:2). So, some of our lack has exhausted their stay because we failed to communicate our needs to God. All this is written to emphasize the point that communication is key. One of the key principles in the eradication of anger and unforgiveness is to communicate to the person or people who committed the offense, but don't attack them or verbally abuse them, but rather let them know that what they did to you was wrong (given it was), and that you were not happy with it. Here are a few ways.

❖ Talk to them privately(preferably). If an incident occurs, and you get angry, and you happen to be in public, tell them you want to talk in private, and if they agree, you can go to a more remote location, and reveal your feelings of anger and disappointment to them.

❖ Ask them not to repeat it again to you (please be polite in this gesture). It is very important to let them know that you don't like those kinds of behaviors, and so doing it will only get you angry again, so inform them not to do it again, or at least not when you're around.

❖ Come to a resolution that same day. It is very important that you come to a resolution that same day. In order for this to happen, they will have to apologize. And if they don't, you may discern to see if there's any form of regret from their behavior. But whatever it may be, as long as it is a righteous way of resolving a conflict, make sure both parties come to a general consensus, and even if you don't receive an apology, if you discern some sort of repentance from the other party, you may take it as a sign of resolution. Some of you may also feel better just telling them about their fault, this is very good. Just let them know about it, this will clear your heart from the weight of such a problem.

Antidote of prayer:

Now, there was a time, someone offended when I was younger, and I remember being very angry at that person. I was sitting In a chair full of anger, and the Holy Spirit gave me an impression to pray in the spirit (in tongues). Now, I had never prayed in tongues whilst I was angry before, in fact that was one of the last things on my mind, and so when I was led to do that, I began. Then I noticed something strange. After a few seconds of praying in tongues, I started feeling better, then after a few minutes, the anger was completely gone. I was marveled at the new discovery that praying in the spirit can help remove anger and unforgiveness from the heart. Now, of course I was led to do this, and so because I was led to do this, I cannot be completely valid in making this a practice with a definite outcome, but I can surely suggest it.

❖ Begin by praying in your understanding. Now, whenever you get angry, wait till you calm down, and if you don't feel like talking to the person instantly, or you can't get yourself to do it, what you can do is to ask God to help you forgive them of their offense. And if you can pray in the spirit, after you get angry, you can begin to pray in the spirit. You may not feel like praying at this time of anger, both in the spirit or in your understanding, but try to. Make sure to communicate with God about it. If you want to wait a bit for the anger to go down, then feel free, but make sure to talk it out with God if you can't talk it out with the person/people immediately. Prayer will also work if this is a matter that can't be talked out for whatever reason. There may be some special circumstances in which you may not be able to talk it out with those that made you angry, so in such cases, communicating with God is key, either in the spirit(tongues) or in your understanding.

Immunity:

Now when it comes to anger, it is not within my current scope of knowledge accessible to provide an immunity. I think in most scenarios (if not all), anger is inevitable. Even God himself gets angry, he's just slow to it, and that is how we ought to be. Because there indeed comes a time where one's tolerance for certain things is outlived, and therefore resulting in an outburst of an emotion we know as anger or offense. It is the prolongment of this outburst and offense that gives birth to unforgiveness. So, I can only provide you immunities in the sense that they will reduce your likelihood of taking offense, and therefore preventing unforgiveness, but in this case, the possibility of preventing unforgiveness completely for human beings in my opinion is low but not impossible. So, I will only list things that will reduce the likelihood of holding unforgiveness in your heart, preventing it from happening in the first place. Again, it is difficult to prevent offense but it is not impossible, otherwise Jesus would not have commanded us to forgive others. So here are some things you can do to prevent yourself from holding unforgiveness in your heart.

Immunity of Love:
It is written in the word of God that love covers wrong doings. So, in order to reduce the chance of holding unforgiveness in our heart, we must strive

to increase our love for people. It is in increasing our Love for people that we are less likely to hold a grudge for long against them. In order to grow in love for people, we must first grow in love for God. You may come to find that when you grow in love for God, you will naturally love people as well. When you love God, you will want to do what you can to please him, so because of that, you will naturally do what you can to help others as God wishes. So, taking the Love of God, and giving it to others will help reduce the likely hood of unforgiveness, because it is because of the love of God that our sins are able to be forgiven, and that we are able to be saved through our Lord Jesus Christ.

❖ Spend time with God. To grow in love with man, you must grow in love with God, and to grow in love with God, you must spend time with him. Do you know why (ideally) you love your family more than a stranger you just met? Because you've spent much more time with your family than the stranger. So, you know your family and they know you. You have bonds with them that have lasted for long. This is how love is established, through consistent and active intimacy. So, you must indeed spend time with God to build a relationship with him. After spending time with God, your love will grow for him, and you will then grow in love with man and when you grow in love with man, you will find it difficult to hold offense against people but not necessarily to get offended.

Immunity of Discernment:

It is written, "For we wrestle not against flesh and blood, but against principalities, against powers, against the rulers of the darkness of this world, against spiritual wickedness in high places" (Ephesians 6:12). Now, what we need to know is, these evil entities are spirits without bodies. So, because these beings are spirits, but have no bodies to legally operate on earth, they seek to possess bodies, and if they can't possess bodies, they will oppress them. When God created the earth, he made it a requirement for a spirit to have a body in order to operate on earth. So, God created our spirits, then formed our bodies, and blew our spirits into our bodies, so we can operate both in the spiritual and here in the physical. But demons are spirits without bodies to operate on earth, so in order to express themselves here, they find ways to possess a human or animal body to find expression. Luckily for us as believers of Jesus Christ, demons no longer have the authority to possess us, but they can indeed oppress us, but only if through ignorance we do not keep them from doing so or cast them out. Now, the reason this was brought up is because, sometimes, the devil can use people for his agenda, and it doesn't necessarily mean those people are of the devil, but maybe they may have been an appropriate and available candidate to be used by the devil as the serpent was in the time of Adam and Eve. It was in Luke that Jesus made known to Simon that the devil sought to have him, but Jesus prayed to reverse that. So sometimes, because of lack of prayer, people may become vulnerable for the exploitation and usage of the devil. Now it is important to note that, when Jesus was to be crucified and they were spitting on him, and insulting him, nailing him to the cross, Jesus said something spectacular. It is written that Jesus said, "Father, forgive them, for they do not know what they are doing" (Luke 23:34). So, we see here that it is possible for people to do certain things with the belief that they are performing an action for a reason, but rather in God's perceptive truth (which is our true reality), they are doing something else. So, these people crucified Jesus thinking he was a wrong doer, not knowing they were killing an innocent man, and rather setting him free, so that he could set us free in the end. You see, the devil thought killing Jesus would prevent him from fulfilling destiny, but it was indeed God's plan that he should die, so that we could live. God used the devil to fulfill his plan. So, the devil used man to persecute his intentions, and Jesus knew this, that is why he asked God-the father to forgive them because they knew not that they were being used to fulfill a plan and a purpose. So, when you see people act strangely towards you sometimes, don't be quick to get angry, you need to understand that the devil may be using them to get at you. Maybe God wants to use someone to help you with something you've been praying for, but because you could not discern that person, you acted mean and rude to them, and because of that, your need has not been met, and you keep thinking God has not answered you, but you failed to realize he answered you by bringing that person into your life, but because of some sort of conflict, the relationship was ruined, and you weren't able to get your breakthrough. Sometimes, that's how the devil attacks your breakthrough. He may use the person God has chosen for you to provoke you to anger, and if you lack discernment and act in the flesh to react in anger, you will ruin and prevent your own breakthrough, so please, discern, and be slow to anger as our God is, for you know not the agent God has assigned to get you to your next level.

❖ You must grow in discernment. In order to be more discerning, you must grow in it. In order to grow and sharpen your discernment, you must pray frequently, and preferably in the spirit. Praying in the spirit is one of the fastest ways to sharpen your spirit, and therefore sharpen your discernment to spiritual things. Of course, if you can't pray in the spirit, pray in your understanding, and ask God to sharpen your discernment. It is very important that you also read the word of God. Doing this will also help you grow in discernment.

The Cure

Premature Death(PD)

___

Recipients:

This represents the specific entity of our being that may be affected by the problem of PD.

|| Spirit - Soul - **Body**

Area of Focus:

This represents the specific entity we will focus on providing the immunity to prevent.

|| Premature Death of the Body

Category:

Place, Operation, Companionship

Immunity:

Given the context of this topic, we will only discuss immunities and not antidotes because the dead are inactive. Now, it is written in the word of God that we all have our days numbered and measured. God brought us to earth to execute his will, and he gave us a set time to do it, but sometimes the devil may try to cut that time short, and because of the ignorance of God's people, the devil may end up succeeding in his quest, moving that

___

mandate to someone else. But it is my prayer that none of you after reading this will be part of those the devil succeeds in killing premature in Jesus Name. Now before I begin to discuss more on this issue, it is wise to explain where death came from and why it exists. You see, when God made man (both male and female), he made man for a reason. God does not waste, he fulfils. So, man was created under the law of fulfillment, meaning man's existence was for a particular execution. But before God made man, he created the earth for man to inhabit, and creation was in existence(earth) to assist man in his (both male and female) execution. So, creation was created to assist man's life on earth. So as long as man was fulfilling what he was created to do, creation will fulfill what it was created to do, which is to help man live his God ordained life. Now, what happened was that God created man to depend on him for knowledge. This is because God created man to function out of knowledge, and so God made man to depend on knowledge for survival, and he wanted himself (God) to be the only source of knowledge man will receive from, since he created Man in the first place. Now, after God had made man, he planted a garden and put the man in the garden. Then he commanded the man not to eat of the tree of knowledge of good and evil, why? Because God did not create man to do evil, neither did he create man to know "good" apart from him. This means man would no longer need God to do anything because they know what good is and they can do it without him. So, since man does things as a result of knowledge, if man should eat that fruit, man will gain knowledge of evil, therefore man would now be able to do evil, and this was never God's plan. So, eating this fruit would allow man to maximize their free will in the scope of choice of action. So, there were several trees there with fruits that had more implications than satisfying physical hunger, which in the presence of God, is not much of a problem. So, God instructed the man to keep his garden, and made known to him what fruits he and his wife (Eve) could and couldn't eat. And the only tree God told them not to eat out of was the tree of the knowledge of good and evil. Now, because man was created to depend on knowledge in order to perform an action, the devil came in to use this to his advantage. You see, in order to operate on the earth, you need a body. Spirits cannot operate on earth without physical bodies to assist in their executions. Because the devil is a spirit, he had to get a body to execute his negative and evil agenda. So, he had to find a creature that had the abilities he could use to appropriately execute his intentions successfully. So, he found the serpent to be his best bet. So, he used the serpent's body to operate on earth, to communicate "a knowledge" to the woman, and it was out of curiosity for more knowledge that the woman took the fruit and ate it and gave it to her husband to eat it as well. This is what I explained earlier. Man does things as a result of knowledge. It was the devil's knowledge that caused man to sin (by eating the fruit). It was after this action that man (both male and female) had committed what we know as sin. Sin is simply doing against what the creator created you to do. Doing against the will of the creator (God). So, because of this act, man came into a knowledge that man was not supposed to come into, the knowledge of good (apart from God) and evil (against the nature of God). And after sin, a new candidate arose, this is what we called death. God did not intend death to be man's portion originally. Now, since God created man to live for a reason, he created the earth and things in it to assist man in living so that man can fulfill the reason for his (both male and female) life. But now that man rebelled against God, they no longer sought to fulfill the will of God, this means that man's reason for living was not being prosecuted. This means, man's life became useless in the sense that man chose to do against what they were told to do by their creator (God). So, if man's life was no longer used for what it was created for, then man no longer had a place in life. And because creation existed to help man live in order to prosecute

God's will, but man chose not to use their life for what it was created for, creation would no longer assist man in living, but will rather work to expel man from life on earth. As long as man uses his (male and female) life for what it was created for, creation will assist man in living that life, but as long as man no longer wants to use their life for what it was made for, man would be in waste. This means, man no longer has business in life, so man will have to die because man's life is no longer useful. So as opposed to helping man live, creation will now have to help man die because as opposed to using their life for what it was meant for (God's will), man used it for something else (sin, rebellion, man's desires). Creation can only do what it was created for, or the opposite of that. Now, creation had a contingency in operation. So, in order for creation to operate properly, man must operate properly. But if man does not operate properly, creation must still operate, but creation must do the opposite of what it was created to do because the contingency placed on its operation mandate was not being met. This is the reason for death. So, the animals that were never created to hurt man could now attack and kill man. The ocean and the sea that was never intended to hurt man could now cause man to sink, bringing death. Food man was never supposed to need to eat became a gateway for many diseases and illnesses to invade man's body. Creation reacted to man's rebellion, therefore bringing man's life closer and closer to death, because man was not using his (male and female) life for what it was created for (the will of God), but man rather wanted to use his(male and female) life for his(male and female) own pleasure and purposes. So, when Jesus our Lord came to earth, he showed us a glimpse of what our lives could've been like on earth without sin. He walked on water and did not sink, because creation was created to help man live as long as man was using his life for the will of his creator. So, because Jesus was doing the perfect will of God and had no sin, the sea could not cause Jesus to drown, so it had to hold him up. Jesus went to fast in the wilderness with the wild beasts, and yet they did him no harm because he was using his life for what it was brought to earth for, so animals could bring him no harm. So, when it comes to premature death, it's linked to mainly two things. Your life source through the portal of earth(parents) and fulfilling the will of God for your life.

Immunity of Parental Honor:

It is written, "Honor your father and your mother, so that you may live long in the land the Lord your God is giving you" (Exodus 20:12). So, part of what helps you live longer is when you honor your parents. They were chosen by God to aid the manifestation of your birth on earth, therefore your life span on earth can be affected by them. The word honor here means to treat with respect. You may disagree with them, or they may have done something against you that you don't like, but disrespecting them, disgracing them, insulting them and reacting to them in a dishonoring way will not help you live long. You must remember that your parents can affect your life span. So even if you don't get along with them, do not dishonor them. You can stay away, but make sure before you refrain from them, you leave things on a good note, this is very important. Many people are having life threatening challenges because they have dishonored their parents, and you'll be astonished that such a serious life-threatening issue can be resolved and healed with a simple apology, and forgiveness from parents. Here are some ways to honor your parents.

❖ Never Insult them. Please read this carefully, and they that have wisdom, let them heed to my counsel. It matters not how angry your parents may make you, if you are wise, you'll never insult them from now on, both in their presence or not. Never insult your parents, because this can give the devil occasion to tamper with your life on earth. Speaking negative words of insult to your parents may only backfire back on you, so be wise, and refrain from this.

❖ Make sure your parents are taken care of. You must make sure that even if you're not close with your parents, make sure they are safe. Make sure they have a roof over their head, and they have food to eat and water to drink(I don't just mean this literally, but if there's a life threatening need in their life, and you have the power to solve it without life threatening consequences to you or others, please help them fulfill their need). Make sure you honor them by taking care of their needs in some way. Doing this is considered honoring them. Not taking care of your parents and leaving their needs unmet when you have the capacity to do it is considered dishonor. So read this carefully, God is speaking to you right now through this book. If you've not been close with your parents, and you've not been taken care of them, call them, find them, and get things right. You may come to find that some of your issues are tied to your unresolved situations with your parents. And if you hold anything against your parents, let it go now.

❖ Seek their forgiveness. You may come to find that even after years have passed since a conflict may have occurred, parents may still be holding a grudge against their kids. Read these words o ye wise ones and obey my counsel in the prolongment of your lives. Sometimes, just by the mere fact that one or more of your parents are holding a grudge of unforgiveness against you, it may cause certain life complications. Here's what you need to do. You must find a way to get with your parents (given their still alive) and ask them (given you are no longer living with them) if there's any unsettled matter they should know about. Ask them if they have a problem with you now, or something you did in the past that they may still be holding on to as an offense. Then ask them to forgive you. Settle the matter with them. Apologize, and honor them. Make sure you get their true and sincere forgiveness; you may be surprised at what you may find. You may be shocked to find certain complications in your life will be no more.

Immunity of the Spirit of Wisdom:

Now, it is written, "Joyful is the person who finds wisdom, the one who gains understanding. For wisdom is more profitable than silver, and her wages are better than gold. Wisdom is more precious than rubies; nothing you desire can compare with her. She offers you long life in her right hand, and riches and honor in her left (Proverbs 3:13-16). Now, it is written here that he (male and female) who finds wisdom, has received an offer to have long life. So, one of the keys to long life, is to have wisdom. So, make it a prayer that God should give you wisdom. Pray for the spirit of Wisdom to be manifest in your life. Having wisdom in operation in every aspect of your life will ensure that your life is lived wisely, and therefore righteously, and therefore long and fulfilled. Now, here's a bit of insight in the topic of wisdom pertaining to long life. If you have the spirit of wisdom, you will become more prudent. This means, you will think of the future consequences and benefits of your pending actions way more before you come to a resolute conclusion. So, if you're tempted to smoke, and you've been given the spirit of wisdom, prudence will bring it to your understanding that, if you perform such an action, your lungs will be at risk for disfunction, and therefore it is likely your lifespan may be reduced as a result of an illness that may occur because of such an action, so after prudence brings the potential consequence of this action to your understanding, wisdom will then advice you against such action, and if you are indeed wise, you will refrain from smoking. If you are tempted to text or be on your phone whilst driving, then prudence will bring to your understanding the potential for an accident to occur because of your divided attention towards a task that requires your full attention. After prudence makes it known to you that it is possible for your eyes to be on the phone and by the time you raise your eyes back to your front view, a car may be seconds from hitting you on the driver side, therefore causing potential death, wisdom will then advice you to put the phone down and focus your attention on the road, and if you indeed listen and obey, you will then be much safer. Remember, the spirit of wisdom is one of the spirits of God. It is God's wisdom, personified. It is God-dimension wisdom. So, I urge you, pray for the spirit of wisdom, that you may be wise in your dealings and live long upon the face of the earth.

Immunity of Impartation:
Now we have to understand that in the kingdom of God, everybody carries a different dimension of God. Some carry the healing dimension, others the prophetic, and some the administrative, some the wisdom, and others the financial dimension. We need to understand that once a person has attained a specific dimension of God, or an anointing, they have the ability to impart it unto someone. A dimension of this is called learning. Someone knows something we don't, and because of that they are able to do something we can't. So, they teach those who can't do what they can, and suddenly, what others couldn't do before can now be achieved because they learned it from someone who could do it already. Now, when it comes to long life, be informed that there are people that have the grace to live. It maybe in their family line, that people from that family generally live long. If you meet

someone who has an established line of living long, meaning their family members generally live long, and you happen to meet this person at an unusually old age, yet they don't express many symptoms of old age, meaning they walk with their two feet without support, and they exhibit strength as though they were younger, then this may be an appropriate candidate for impartation. Now please make sure that before you do this, you discern that the heritage of long life from such people is truly a grace from God and not a result of evil doings. Once you've discerned such a grace from God on a person to live long, you may ask them to pray for you (please make sure they are Christian), and also be led by the spirit of God. But Ideally, if this person is able to pray for you regarding the impartation of the grace responsible for allowing them to live for such a long time and have such strength and vitality without being killed by sickness or accidents or any of such conflicts, then behold, you also may become a partaker of their grace of long life. Of course, make sure you honor this person or people, it may be that you met a need in their life, or you invested money or resources into their life, but do not go empty handed, it is wise that you go to them with a giving heart.

Immunity of the Will of God:

Now, here's the main way you protect yourself from premature death. You must subscribe your life to do what it was created and intended to do; this is the will of God. Subscribing to the will of God is the easiest way to secure your life on earth by God's protection. As long as your life is useful to God in fulfilling his will, the devil will not be allowed to take you out (given you are not in active sin). So, it is very important that you subscribe your life to the will of God, because doing so will make your life useful, and once your life is useful, God will ensure that you remain on earth to fulfill what you're called to do(ideally). Here are a few ways to subscribe to the will of God for your life.

❖ Ask God. It is very important to communicate with your creator about what you were created for. God knows why you're here, so there's no point playing guess and check, simply ask God. Pray about this. Ask him to reveal it to you, whether through a prophet, or through a dream, or a vision, or his word, or his voice. Ask God to show you why you're here. Pray about this and note that you may not receive an answer immediately, but keep praying, eventually, you will.

❖ Examine your passions. While you're making the will of God a prayer point, your passions and interests may be an indication.

❖ Work in the house of God. I highly recommend working and doing something in the house of God, whilst you figure out your passions and interests as well as praying for the revelation of the will of God. Working in the house of God will help jump start your entrance into destiny and will put you at the right place to discover the will of God for your life.

Sin(General)

Recipients:

This represents the specific entity of our being that may be affected by the problem of PD.

|| Spirit - **Soul** - **Body**

Area of Focus:

This represents the specific entity we will focus on providing the immunity to prevent.

|| Sin of the body and the soul; after salvation, your spirit is saved and becomes one with the spirit of God, so sin in this regard is of the soul and the body.

Category:

Place, Operation, Companionship, Satisfaction

Antidote & Immunity:

Please note: Because of such a broad topic of sin, the antidote and immunities against sin will go hand to hand. They will be both a cure to sin and an immunity to prevent it.

Man's Biggest problem has always been sin. Without sin, things would have been much different. Many have wondered why a God deemed good would allow so many problems. Why would God let people die? Why would he let people fall sick? Why would he allow accidents? Why would he allow poverty? Homelessness? These are questions asked by many, both believers and unbelievers, and I hope reading this book will begin to open your eyes to the answer. It all began with sin. God never intended for man to die. God never intended for creation to malfunction against man. God created man for glory, but sin came to ruin. Now let's discuss a bit more about sin. First what is sin? To understand what it is, we need know what context sin applies to. Now, God created man for a reason. So, God gave man life for a reason. Because man has a creator, man is subject to their creator(God). Now, it just so happened that this creator (God) gave this creation (Man) a will. So, the creator made man with the intention that man will choose to fulfill what he made man to fulfill. Choosing to do the opposite of what man was created to do is what we call sin; that is, doing against the will of the creator. So, you must understand that sin only affects the creation, not the creator. The reason God cannot sin is not because he chooses not to, it is because there is nothing like sin to a creator. You see, in order for the possibility of sin to be applicable to you, you must be created. And since God wasn't created, there's no one for him to sin against. God cannot commit murder because he gave a life, so taking that life back is not murder, that life belongs to him. God cannot lie, because there is nothing like lying to God. What God says becomes truth instantly. So, if someone is clearly 6 feet to us, but God says that individual is 4 feet, that individual will physically change and become 4 feet. I hope you can understand this, God only creates with his words, he doesn't lie. Whatever he says, must happen. So, if something pre-exists as something else, and God says it's another, then that something else will instantly become another, because God cannot lie.

His words will become truth to support and guard his reputation. So, sin is only a substance of creation. Now, sin became abundant once Man ate of the tree of the knowledge of good and evil. The cause of many problems has been the knowledge of evil, of which God commanded man not to eat. You see, God did not create man to know how to do evil, because he made man a subject of knowledge, and so as long as man knows, man has the potential to do. Now, God knows that there are such things called evil, and he did not want man to be associated with them. But since that knowledge existed, it must be present along with other things such as the tree of life. So as long as man does not touch this knowledge, even though it exists, man will be fine. But the moment man eats of this fruit, man will acquire a knowledge of evil, as well as good. So, man will have a balanced knowledge bank, therefore man will no longer need God, because man now knows what good is, and what evil is. But the case here is, when man comes to the knowledge of evil, they will now have the ability to do it, and God did not want man to do evil. God did not even want man to know about such a knowledge. God did not want man to know how to do things like murder. God did not want man to know how to do things like committing adultery, which is having intercourse with another's spouse. God did not want man to know how to do things like lying (speaking against the truth). God did not want man to know how to do things like stealing. These are all examples of evil doings, and God knew if man should come into such a knowledge, they will make themselves subject to such evil, and when they do these things, it will cause all sorts of problems. This is the reason for all our problems. Subjecting ourselves to such a knowledge of good (apart from God) and evil (against the will and nature of God). This is why God commanded the man to stay away from this tree, and the first thing that happened when man ate the fruit was, they were afraid. So, fear came in, then they were ashamed of their nakedness, so shame came in. And they were kicked out of the garden, so misplacement came in. So, one sin was committed, and the sin that was committed was no ordinary sin. It was a sin of eating out of a tree that will impart a knowledge of how to commit various types of sin(s) (by experience). So, sin was what gave birth to our problems. You may come to find that even after giving our life to Christ, the devil can use the sins in our lives to legally bring destruction to us. Here's the thing. Once an individual give's their life to Christ, meaning, to begin the journey of salvation through Christ Jesus, God gives that individual grace to overcome sin. This grace to overcome sin is provided by his spirit, the Holy Spirit. It is through the Holy Spirit that we are able to receive grace to live a righteous life. We cannot live a righteous life with our own strength, that was proven unfeasible by the law, that is why Jesus was brought to die, so that we may partake of his eternal life. He became a role model for us. Jesus was someone who indeed lived a righteous life and so by his power, we to are able to live a righteous life. So, after sin eroded the earth and brought death, if man would die, God would not have been able to prosecute his originally intended will for man, because after man would die out of earth, man's soul will not exist in life, but rather in death because the law of sin and death is multi-dimensional. Anyone that sins in time will die out of time and spend eternity in death. And anyone that sins in eternity cannot fail to exist, so they will exist in eternal death, which is eternal fire. Now, what happened was this. Man existed on earth, and earth exists in the realm of time. So, when man sinned and got a death sentence, man would exit from earth, but man is an eternal creature, so man would have to continue to exist. But since man had the ability to choose to use their life for what God intended it for (his will) or to use their life for what they want (man's will), man became subject to judgment-scripture reference (Hebrew 9:27). So, man would have to be judged after life on earth before their eternal destination is assumed. So, a place was made for man to exist before judgement, a place of death. Now since God did not want man to exist in death, but rather in life with him, God was motivated by love to rescue the human race. And so, God had to find a way by wisdom, to rescue the human race. Now since this project had to do with allowing a sinner to live, even though a sinner's portion is death, God would have to find a way to get a righteous person to die, even though a righteous person's portion is life. If God could get a righteous person to die illegally, then it will become legal for a sinner to live in order to balance out that equation. In other words, God expressed his wisdom in legalities. He knew a sinner must die but he wanted his people to live even though all had sinned. So, if he should allow sinners to live without legal cause, it will be unjust. It will cause conflict, and issues. It will cause an imbalance. It will be against his word. So, to get his people to live, he had to allow the opposite to happen. A righteous person must die. But how is this possible? It is as impossible as getting a sinner to live, but yet God found a way. He was able to make an illegality a legality, praise God for his Wisdom responsible for creating this path. The path for a sinner to live and not die. So, it is by wisdom that God found a way to prosecute such a wise plan. What you need to know is that God put the spirits of man in Adam to carry as sperm, and he put the bodies in Eve to carry as eggs. So, when Adam sinned, it affected the life force of man, so man inherited sin through Adam. So, no one in the human race had righteous life because when Adam sinned, he sinned with the spirits of Man in him as sperm, so we all inherited this sin. Now, here's what you need to know about the law of sin and death. It was through Adam that our life became contaminated with sin, and through eve that we would pay for our sin by death (of the earthly body). So, God decided he would come to earth himself through his own seed of righteousness, but he would use a human body so that he could still die for the sins of man, but this way, because he is in a body that was cursed to die as a result of sin, but his life force (which is the seed) had no sin, he would be guiltless of death, therefore through this illegal death, sinners will also be able to live(legally). So, God seeded himself so that he could fulfill the righteousness aspect of his plan, and he was born out of a woman so that his body could still die but not for any inherited sin of Adam or his own sin. So, Jesus was born a righteous human with a body that had the ability to die, and he was wrongly accused, and he was killed. Now, since it was illegal for a righteous human to die yet it still happened, because Jesus did not belong in death, God raised him from the dead. And because a righteous person died, God could allow sinners to live through Jesus Christ by the power that raised him from the dead, The Spirit of God. So now, the way to life and to the father, is through he who made it possible for us to live and exist in life, through our Lord Jesus Christ. So, once you're a believer, God made possible to overcome sin through his Spirit. So, a believer still struggling with sin, is a believer who hasn't been able to appropriately utilize the provision God has made available, and I pray as you read this book, and practice what I teach you here, sin will become less and less of a problem for you in Jesus Name.

Antidote of the presence of God:

I remember the first time I fully prayed in the spirit. It was in my freshman dorm at the University, and that day, I felt a starring in my chest, and I felt very emotional like I wanted to cry (did not feel sad) but didn't know why. So, as it was my custom, I prayed that day in my understanding because I could not pray in the Spirit fully even though I had been baptized with water and baptized in the Holy Spirit. So, this particular day, I kneeled down to pray as it was a daily practice for me at that time, and I usually prayed for about 20 or so minutes, not that I was counting but after I would finish and I would go on my phone, it seemed that was the average. So, as I prayed this faithful Saturday, something new happened. I realized that as I was praying, I was being pulled in and in more into God's presence, and I noticed that I opened my mouth to pray in the spirit, and behold I was speaking in tongues, and crying and feeling the presence of God in such a way that I had not felt until that time. That was the first time I had prayed for over 1 hour, and that was my first experience with the presence of God in such a manner. That was the first time I cried in the presence of God without boundaries. His presence was so saturating, that I cried as I prayed and worshiped in the secret place. And after I came out of that experience, it was as if whatever was causing me to sin or luring me to sin had left, and I felt so close to God that sin was not an interest of mine, and righteousness became the interest of my thirst. Since that time, a hunger was birthed in me for God, and I prayed in the spirit every day for no less than 1 hour. Most days it was 2 hours, others it was 3. This was the beginning of my call. You see, in prayer, there are realms we must climb to. When you begin to pray, you may initially be distracted, but there is a realm you get to, that you touch the presence of God through prayer, and you know you've reached this realm when your concentration is no longer about yourself but about God. There is a realm much higher, after reaching this realm, your body may experience some changes, for me, this was when I began to cry. I also began to be more distinct in praying in tongues, I also got a bit louder. This is the realm we reach, that causes those demons that like to whisper thoughts of evil in our minds to cease and to flee. So how do we enter this realm? We can do this through prayer, and through worship. Please note: the decision to pull you into this realm is completely on God. Remember, he is a sovereign God. He is the God King. He is King God. So, he is responsible for quickening you, but the ways I listed are there to prepare you and to show him that you are indeed hungry for an experience in his presence.

❖ Begin by finding a private and secure place. It is very important for you to understand that if you want to get in the presence of God through prayer and worship, you must worship him in spirit and in truth as it is written in the word. You must give him all of your heart not some. The easiest way to do that is to remove yourself from distraction. I advise that you get yourself in a room and lock the door and make sure no one is around that could potentially cause a distraction. I usually like to go a place where I'm completely alone, to eliminate any possibility of a distraction, because I know how important the presence of God is, and just one encounter may set me free from a lifetime of problems. So, make sure you're alone, and put your phone on silent, as well as other distractions, this time is for God.

❖ Worship God. I find it very helpful to play worship music while praying. Of course, before you begin to pray, you may find it helpful to just thank God, and worship him. After doing so, you may find it even more helpful to play worship music to help you concentrate on God. I find this very helpful. So, play powerful Christian songs or strings of worship that will help you pray and concentrate enough to get into the presence of God without distraction. You can also worship without music if you prefer that.

❖ Begin to pray. I usually pray about 98% in the spirit, and the other 2% with my understanding. That's usually how I handle my prayer life. I do understand that some of you reading this may not be able to pray in the spirit, and so in that scenario, pray with your understanding, or simply, sing songs of worship to God, whereby you climb into his presence, and when he invites you in, you indeed will become free from the demonic pressures to sin, and you'll enjoy the sovereign presence of He who is I am, He who is Lord, He that occupies the office of God. So, if you can pray in the spirit, I advise you to do so after securing a private place.

❖ Stay Connected. Please note, that after you begin to pray, your mind may begin to drift. You may begin to think about some things in your life, and things you need to get done, etc... Again, make sure to erase all those things from your mind during this time of prayer. You must make sure to stay connected. This is why I personally play music to help me, especially when I first begin. Now make sure there's nothing holding you back. When you begin to pray, you must do it with all your heart. So, it is important to clear all your worries during this time and focus completely on the prayer. If dimming the lights help, then so be it, or if you'd like to pray in the dark, then so be it, but whatever is safe, legal and righteous for you to do in order to be completely focused on God, please do.

❖ Endure. After staying completely focused on prayer (being that it is in the spirit), you may notice that your tongues may begin to sound more precise, and that you may even get louder in speaking in tongues. This is good, these are all signs that you're ascending. After some time in this, you will notice that you're completely focused on God, and that your worries are no longer a concern, then you may notice you may become what I describe as emotional. This is good, you're enjoying the presence of God, don't cut this short. Stay in the presence for as long as you can. After you're done praying, you may notice that you're calmer. You may notice that the urge to sin has been silenced. This is good. If you are able to enter the presence frequently, you'll notice that sin will become less and less of a problem, and eventually, you may no longer find sin as a difficulty in your life anymore, this is my prayer for you In Jesus name, that indeed your thirst for righteousness will be filled and quenched.

Antidote of fasting and prayer:

You must come to the understanding that the fastest way to quench the appetites of the flesh is to fast. Now, I understand that not everybody is a fan of fasting, and I also understand that there are different and several types of fasts. But the ideologies will be able to be applied to the various common types.

❖ Fasting the eyes and ears (Filtered Fasting). This to me is what I intend to spend all my time doing, not just a particular time in my life. You see, this type of fasting simply involves preventing your eyes and ears from seeing and hearing negative things. It is important that you do this long enough for you to be able to hear something unrighteous from someone else and it won't be powerful enough to affect you. Here's what I mean. This type of filtration system is quite simple, but you may find it difficult to do at first. All you must do is simple, stop watching shows and movies that have sinful things in them such as cussing, sexual immorality, etc… Limit what you see to non-sexual things. This doesn't mean you can't watch movies from the world but don't let your eyes see sinful things. This is because once you've seen it; the enemy can use that to lure you to commit it. You'll realize that those who are bound by lust and immorality began by watching contents with such sinful acts in them. And it was through that, the devil was able to manifest those actions in their lives. So please, do not watch shows and movies with sinful things, especially sexual and immoral things. If you can't do this constantly, then start with a week at a time, and move up. Secondly, you must keep your ears from hearing things that are sinful. Start with the kind of music you listen to. Refrain from listening to music that have cuss words, sexually immoral references, and such. Again, this does not mean only listen to Christian music, but make sure that what you listen to does not promote sin. So again, you can do this for a week, and see how it goes, then you can keep extending it until it eventually becomes your lifestyle, you'll notice that sin may become less and less of a problem for you.

❖ Regular Fasting. Of course, you may be aware of the regular type of fasting, which is done in various ways. Generally, the quickest and most powerful way to suppress the tendency to sin is truly to fast, pray and read the word. Of course, when fasting, you are to refrain from food, and sometimes depending on the type of fasting you're engaged with, you may eat light food, once a day (that is to break your fast), and you may also drink. Some fasts are called dry fasts. And those are done without food. Now depending on the type of fasts you are used to engaging in or you would like to engage, I will simply create a general platform of things you can do to maximize your fasting. While fasting, of course it is important to pray. But pray for longer hours than you do when you're not fasting. This is because long prayers mixed with fasting goes a long way. So as a personal example, if my daily prayer life happens to be 2 hours, during a fast, my daily prayers will be no less than 4 hours, which is double. I will usually go for 8 hours, but these are not requirements, just references. The second thing to do, is to read the bible, and read it more. It is important to read the word when fasting, because this will be a great source of food for your spirit whilst you're charging it by prayer and starving the flesh by fasting. It is also important that, if at all you engage in entertainment such as watching tv during your fast or after you break your fast, it is very important to stay away from things you usually like doing. If at all you must watch something, let it be a sermon, or a teaching or preaching that will mature you about the things of Christ. So, I will highlight what you need to focus on doing when fasting and praying to maximize this time with God, and to properly eliminate sin.

- Make sure to pray longer during a fast
- Make sure to read and meditate on the word (spend time with this)
- For those who break their fasts (keep your eyes and ears on the things of God, listen to sermons and worship music only)
- When the fasting period is over, practice the Filtering fasting system I discussed previously

Antidote of continues worship and consistent Prayer:

Frequent prayer in the spirit, especially for a good amount of time (daily) will certainly help keep your spirit above the balance of the flesh, therefore making the willingness to sin liable to thoughtful approval. So, for those who can pray in the spirit. If you want to handle sin, you can begin by praying in the spirit for about 30 minutes. If you can't make this, go for as long as you can, and if 30 minutes if too small, you may increase, but remember, this is not about numbers it is about consistency. Make sure to do this each day, you may see a better defense against sin working in your life after some time.

Frequent Worship will also help with sin prevention and elimination. Those spirits responsible for luring you to sin will find themselves away from you when you begin to worship into the presence of Elohim. Find private time, play a powerful Christian song that you like, and begin to worship God. Just do it for a few minutes, over and over again without distraction. Do this every day for a couple of minutes to hours depending on your leading, you'll notice that sin may not be as hard to avoid as you thought.

The Cure

You have come to the end of the book.

If you happen to be reading this book and you have not given your life to Jesus Christ and would like to, or if you gave your life to Christ but you began to drift away into sin, and would love to rededicate your life to Christ, read the next few pages to do so.

The Cure

Rededication

If the Lord Jesus was once your first love. If he was once your all, your everything, but due to the influence of the flesh, you have gone back to your own ways, or if God has become second or third, or he's down below the hierarchy of priorities in your life, and you want to reignite the fire you once had for The Lord. If you want Jesus to become your first Love again, if you want the Spirit of God to begin to lead you, to take over your life, if you want to succeed in failing to gratify the desires of the flesh, if you want to choose Jesus, you want to choose eternal life and forsake the path of eternal destruction, then rededication may be the best choice for you. Please say out loud as a physical manifestation of your inner determination of reignited passion for Jesus, "Lord Jesus, I know I am a sinner, I know I've backslidden, have mercy on me, and forgive my sins, I acknowledge that you are the son of God and you died and rose again on the third day, please come back into my life and be my Lord and personal Savior, reignite that passion I once had for you, and help me to serve you all the days of my life, help me to stay in faith and stay till the end and finish the race In Jesus name I pray, Amen.

Now that you have made an inward decision and an outward declaration of faith to rededicate your life to Christ, don't grow weary, don't fall, find joy in Jesus Christ, love him, be led by his spirit, and finish the race.

E.K. Bempoh

The Cure

Giving your Life to Jesus Christ

———

If you've decided to give your life to Jesus, please say out loud, "Lord Jesus, I believe that you are the son of God, and that you are Lord, I believe you came to earth and died for my sins and rose again. I pray you forgive my sins and write my name in the book of life in Jesus name, Amen". Now you've given your life to Jesus by confessing that He is Lord and believing in your heart that God raised him from the dead according to Romans 10:9, you have begun your salvation process.

Congratulations. Now the question is most likely, "What next?" Well, serving God isn't really complicated, you just have to be good and avoid sin, and walk in Love. Now, there's much more than that but that's the summary. I will advise you to **read the bible**. Any chance you get, read the bible, because you may have many questions, and reading the bible may answer them, it will inform you about God and many more things. The bible is easily accessible, just download the bible app, or go to bible.com. Next, you'll need to **find a church**, there are churches everywhere now, there's most likely some around you, find a praying and worshiping church and attend. Now I urge you in the meantime to have a prayer life, it's not difficult to pray to God. Here's an example, "Lord Jesus, I thank you for today, ..." you can fill in the gap. **Pray** for meaningful things, and I recommend that you add "fulfilling his will in your life" to your prayer. You can pray for anything, just make sure it's not a selfish and an unnecessary prayer. Read this verse, Jesus tells us how to pray; Luke 11:1-5.

Now, giving your life to Jesus is more than just believing and saying. You must repent. And **repentance** requires a changed mindset. You must make up your mind to end all your past sins and **live Holy** and righteous, and to do that you'll need the Holy Spirit. You may ask, who is the Holy Spirit? The Holy Spirit is the spirit of God, the spirit that raised Jesus from the dead, the spirit in Jesus that made it possible for Healings and miracles to occur. The Holy Spirit is here to lead us to Jesus, He's here to help and empower us to fulfill our purpose and destinies in life. The Holy Spirit also convicts of sin and leads us into Holiness and righteousness. You need the Holy Spirit; I advise you to get the **baptism of the Holy Spirit**. Ask your pastor about it, find a church that does this. Now during this process, you may begin to **speak in other languages, in other tongues.** The manifestation of speaking in tongues will empower you if you wish to have it, it is a manifestation of having the baptism of the Holy Spirit. You may get **baptized in water** as well if you wish, in the bible Jesus was, many believers have been, I personally have, so I recommend getting a water baptism as a physical manifestation of your changed mindset and your repentant lifestyle.

Lastly, I encourage you to **serve The Lord Jesus** as much as possible. Find something to do in your church. It doesn't matter what it is, just serve God, because all your services will be recorded in heaven, and God will reward those who faithfully serve him, make sure your motives are right.

For more info, visit www.christglobe.org

Click the "Newly Saved" tab

Download the ebook "After receiving Salvation

Lightning Source UK Ltd.
Milton Keynes UK
UKHW040019031122
411515UK00037B/114